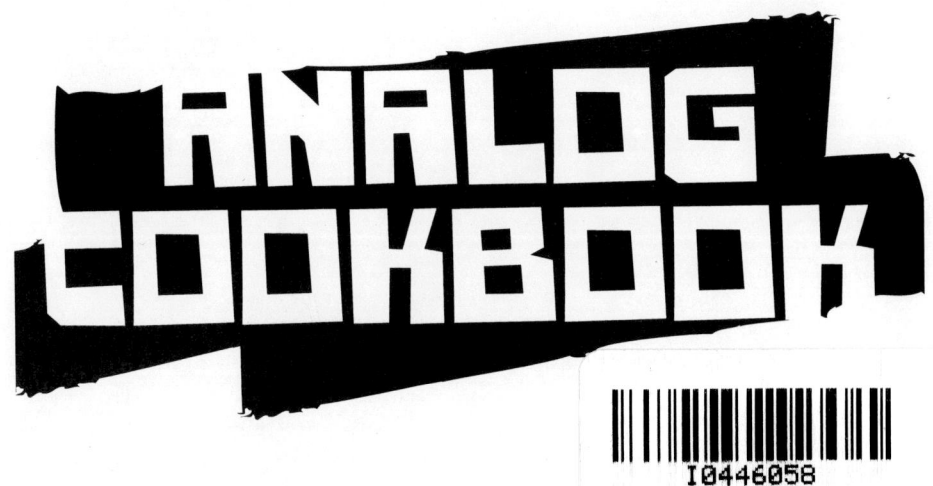

Founder/Editor-in-Chief: Kate E. Hinshaw
Photography editor: Andi Avery
Cover Design by FITZGERALD
Analog Cookbook Logo: Sarah Lawrence Design Emporium

Published by Analog Cookbook © 2020
Submissions and Questions: hello@analogcookbook.com

With generous support by University of Colorado-Boulder:
Department of Cinema Studies & Moving Image Arts

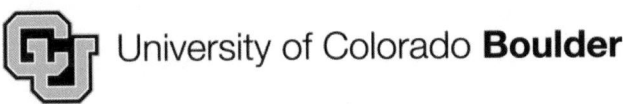

Special Thanks
Jeanne Liotta, Sarah Lawrence, Andi Avery, Spencer Vaughan, FITZGERALD

Letter from the editor

In a perfect world, this letter would be some eloquent and articulated battle cry that compliments the thoughtful discourse filmmakers featured here are grappling with. In reality, I'm scribbling, scratching, and stumbling over words in a notebook on a bumpy flight. I'm reminded of what so many of you have brought up in your recipes, essays, and interviews—analog film is imperfect. Beauty comes from mistakes. It is in the bubbles and scratches, the layers of colors, and grain that we find ourselves. This is why celluloid is effective.

Filmmaker Stefanie Weberhofer has a call for submissions for a project titled *Let's be a Forest* (Pg 25). I love this phrase. As we enter a new decade, the idea of growing together as a film forest feels like reprieve from the narcissism that has plagued us in the 10s. We can resist the idea that in order to get ahead as a filmmaker another one must lose. Instead, we can hold each other up. Consider that the weird gooey films you make are tiny acts of rebellion in a time that demands digital sterility. Consider that the imperfections in your film are deeply human and you are enough.

And submit to Stefanie's call.

--Kate E. Hinshaw

Table of Contents

Artists featured

Sehera Nawaz is a Berlin based analog photography artist, passionate about alternative printing techniques. Specialized in Cyanotypes, she tries to broaden the scope of this environmentally friendly technique. After studying computer science, she researched and published in the field of film rendering and computer graphics. Since 2015 she uses her knowledge, of the behavior of light and cameras, to interpret old analog photo-techniques in a contemporary way. After building an UV enlarger, she developed Cyanotypes on curved glass, playing with the effect of a ghostly shadow behind the print. Using tannins to tone she produces two-colored Cyanotypes, that leave the viewer wondering over the process and show a warm altered reality. Her work was recently published in the book by Christina Z. Anderson (Anderson, Christina Z. Cyanotype: The Blueprint in Contemporary Practice. New York: Focal Press, 2019) and featured in the book on analog photography by André Giogoli: (Analoge Fotografie: Das umfassende Handbuch, Rheinwerk Fotografie, 2019). She regularly teaches Cyanotype workshops in her studio.

Skye Thompson is an Australian filmmaker who has constructed The Sleep Window as the psychic space required for her practice to exist. "The Sleep Window is intended as a limbo space between the conflict of binaries. I like the idea that people who live outside of cities are able to straddle both worlds more easily, we can be quite connected to a different kind of survival that doesn't involve technology as much." Her interests are dream interpretation, decolonization and craftivism/mingei. "Right now I'm comfortable with the idea of Mingei as it is closer to craft, seems to be largely a regional practice that won't fit within a trend and usually serves a function. I'm not sure if I'm allowed to call my work Mingei but it is definitely influenced by that idea."

Michael Fleming is an Amsterdam based visual artist. In essence his work appropriates iconic cultural images, altering them to highlight underlying issues. His 'moving paintings' are primarily made out of found footage, using feature films, advertising and pop-cultural scenes completed into a mesmerising montage of images. Flemings work has been featured in exhibitions and film festivals internationally.

General Treegan is a film editor, producer, experimental and documentary filmmaker, photo lab nerd and lover of small formats based in Mexico since 2003.

Stefanie Weberhofer is an Austrian filmmaker and media artist. She works with Super 8, 16mm and 35mm film and explores various DIY techniques in order to create short films and works for the realm of Expanded Cinema.

Rosalia Parra is a student and pop up owner in Atlanta who shoots on 35mm cameras and makes music videos with super 8 film.

Laura Conway is a filmmaker, DJ, and curator based in Denver, Colorado. Laura's filmmaking practice uses absurdity and surrealism to grapple with the complexities of life in late capitalism. As a DJ and musician, Laura's films operate as visual remixes and often start with music as a centerpoint. Employing whimsy to confront power structures Laura's films navigate a terrain between the grotesque and the sensual, the sonic and the visual, and the cliched and the still-possible.

Nikola Dyulgyarov is an experimenter in science, art, and technology. Nikola's exploration of analog image-making spans over a decade and dozens of formats, processes, and techniques. His motivation comes from a natural curiosity for the physical world and an eagerness to bring together theory and practice in any field. Nikola graduated Rice University with a B.Sc. in Organic Chemistry and a Distinction in the Visual Arts. He continues his darkroom antics in Bulgaria and plans to pursue a career in engineering and education.

Dr. Tish Stringer is an anthropologist, media maker, user and curator of endangered technologies. Tish is passionate about celluloid film production, exhibition and preservation. She is a documentary filmmaker whose films include Al-Mabien / In-between: Iraqi Artists in Exile and Not Lost! Linocut Printing with Artemio Rodriquez and is the founder of Dangerous Media, a Houston-based media production and exhibition company. Tish holds a PhD in anthropology from Rice University; her graduate research and dissertation, Move! Guerrilla Media, Collaborative Modes, and the Tactics of Radical Media Making, focused on radical filmmaking collectives working in and with social movements.

Charlie Mirador is a California born artist and photographer based in San Francisco CA. His book Mirror-Door, a publication of words and photographs from Green Golde Publishing, is due out in upcoming 2020.

Ace McColl is a filmmaker and editor based in Atlanta. Her work leans into the experimental, telling intimate stories around femininity, gender conceptions, and familial dynamics through visceral means. Her award-winning short films have screened nationally and exhibited in galleries across the Southeast. She is an alum of NYU Tisch School of the Arts and FAMU International.

Andrés Porras is a freelance videographer and photographer based out of Calgary, Alberta. He's creatively driven to work with analog mediums because of the tangibility and rawness that they provide. He's shot several projects on Super 8 film including one on Kodak's newly revived Ektachrome stock. He also composes his own soundtracks and features spoken-word components in his films. He shoots and hand develops 35mm still film and is hoping to shoot medium or large format in the future. You can follow his film photography on Instagram @mostlyfilmphotos.

Beth Maciorowski is an artist from the United States with a focus in film photography. Her favorite way to create images is with a little edge and experimentation, always manipulating the film or doing in-camera tricks. Nature is her biggest inspiration and most of the work is autobiographical. Instagram: bethmaciorowski

Max Van Loan is an experimental filmmaker, artist, and former scientist who makes deeply personal artwork. Her 16mm and Super 8mm films often draw inspiration from my own introspection.

Ben Barton is a British poet, who works on paper and film. In 2017, his super 8 film 'Stella Erratica' premiered at the Cannes Film Festival, and has since been shown at over 25 international film festivals. His latest book 'The Hospital' was recently published by Cultured Llama. Find out more at benbarton.co.uk.

Autojektor Analog ruin//experimental filmmaker, UK.

Thomas Paul Wilson is an analog filmmaker.

Caity Arthur is a Brooklyn, NY based filmmaker, editor and photographer. Caity's work is mostly shot on 35mm, 16mm and Super 8 film. As a horror enthusiast and SFX artist her biggest influences are Junji Ito, Dario Argento, Andy Muschietti and Rob Zombie. Caity is focused on creating work that pushes the boundaries in horror and gore.

Dani Smith was born and raised in Sparks, Nevada. She pursued a dual degree in Anthropology and Photography at the University of Nevada, Reno. She then went on to gain her MFA in Experimental and Documentary art at Duke University. Her work focuses on the way people interact with their environments and the containers we build to explore our identities. She has a passion for understanding people and for the ability of media arts to tell stories and influence the way people view the world. She is now currently located in Brooklyn, NY and is focusing on work that looks at her body and chronic pain, alongside making work about urban living and the environment.

Thom Kuo was born in Taipei, Taiwan and raised in Cincinnati, Ohio. Thom has a BFA in Photography from Bowling Green State University and a MFA in film production from Loyola Marymount University. He is currently senior film scanning technician at EFilm in Hollywood, California.

Svava Valdis Tergesen is a photographer and experimental filmmaker currently living and working on unceded Coast Salish territories, also known as Vancouver, BC.

Britany Gunderson is pursuing a BFA in Film, Video, Animation, and New Genres at the University of Wisconsin-Milwaukee. Her practice is often interdisciplinary, creating film and video work that uses material forms such as hand-cut paper, textile fabrics, and celluloid. Exploring ideas of personal non-fiction, her work tries to expand the idea of what a moving image can be. She has screened at venues internationally and received an Honorable Mention at the 2018 Milwaukee Underground Film Festival.

Mona Fani is a mixed media artist and editor living in Vancouver, BC.

Sacred Hatreds is a mixed media artist based in Long Beach, CA, and is currently pursuing a B.A. in Studio Arts with a minor in Entrepreneurship at California State University, Long Beach. Besides her visual art pieces she likes creating studio vlogs on YouTube, and creating memories with her boyfriend, Joe, and their diggy dog, Koda.

Mads Madison is a self taught analog visual artist, he currently lives in Germany. Mads creates upcycled photos for his wasted films project. His philosophy is "reuse, revolt, reclaim, recycle."

Shane Dedman is a non-binary filmmaker based in Atlanta, GA. They produce, write, direct, edit, and vision experimental video art, shorts, and feature length films.

Jess Giacobbe is an artist/filmmaker residing in upstate NY and Founder and Curator of Oscillation Transia Film Festival, a non-profit traveling event hosting free solar powered showcases of independent cinema across the U.S. since 2017.

FITZGERALD is a budding filmmaker, writer, artist, and music head from the South, currently based in Denver, Colorado. He lives with his record player and James Baldwin books. He is currently a BFA candidate at the University of Colorado - Boulder, where he studies Film Production and minors in Ethnic Studies and Studio Art Practices. He aims to tell stories that de/reconstruct masculinity and reorient the gaze on Black bodies, combining his love of movement, music, and design with moving images.He is a (self-proclaimed) Mind Traveler.

Andi Avery was born in New York, where she learned to give her unvarnished opinion on just about everything. After a promising childhood defined by an incorrigible book habit, and 4 years in an intensive acting and directing program, she dropped out of an all-girls private college after 8 months. She spent the next decade trying to assuage her guilt by obtaining as many odd certifications as possible as she tried to find her niche. The yoga teacher-cum-sommelier-cum-wildlife veterinary technician-cum-sex worker (sure, you can add a rim shot in there if you like)-cum-stuntwoman finally pulled her shit together in 2015 when she conceptualized a film based on her experiences in sex work. Leaving Charlie was shot in 2016 by a crew of 40 women & non-binary individuals. The narrative short has made rounds on the festival circuit, landing her 3 awards for her directing. Most importantly, it finally allowed her to utter the only statement that got a bigger eye-roll from Mom & Dad than her job as a stripper: "…but what I really want to do, is direct."

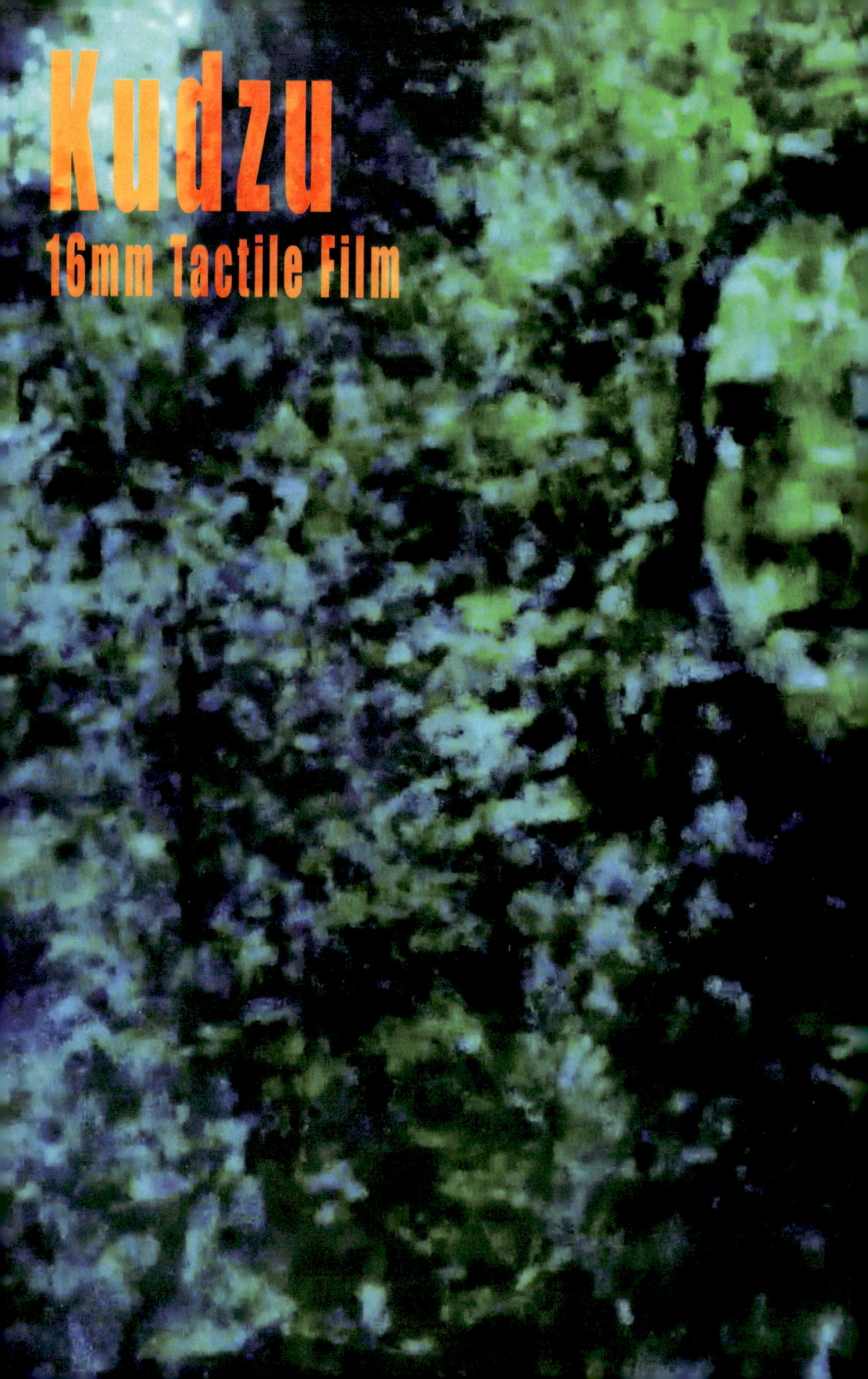

Kudzu
16mm Tactile Film

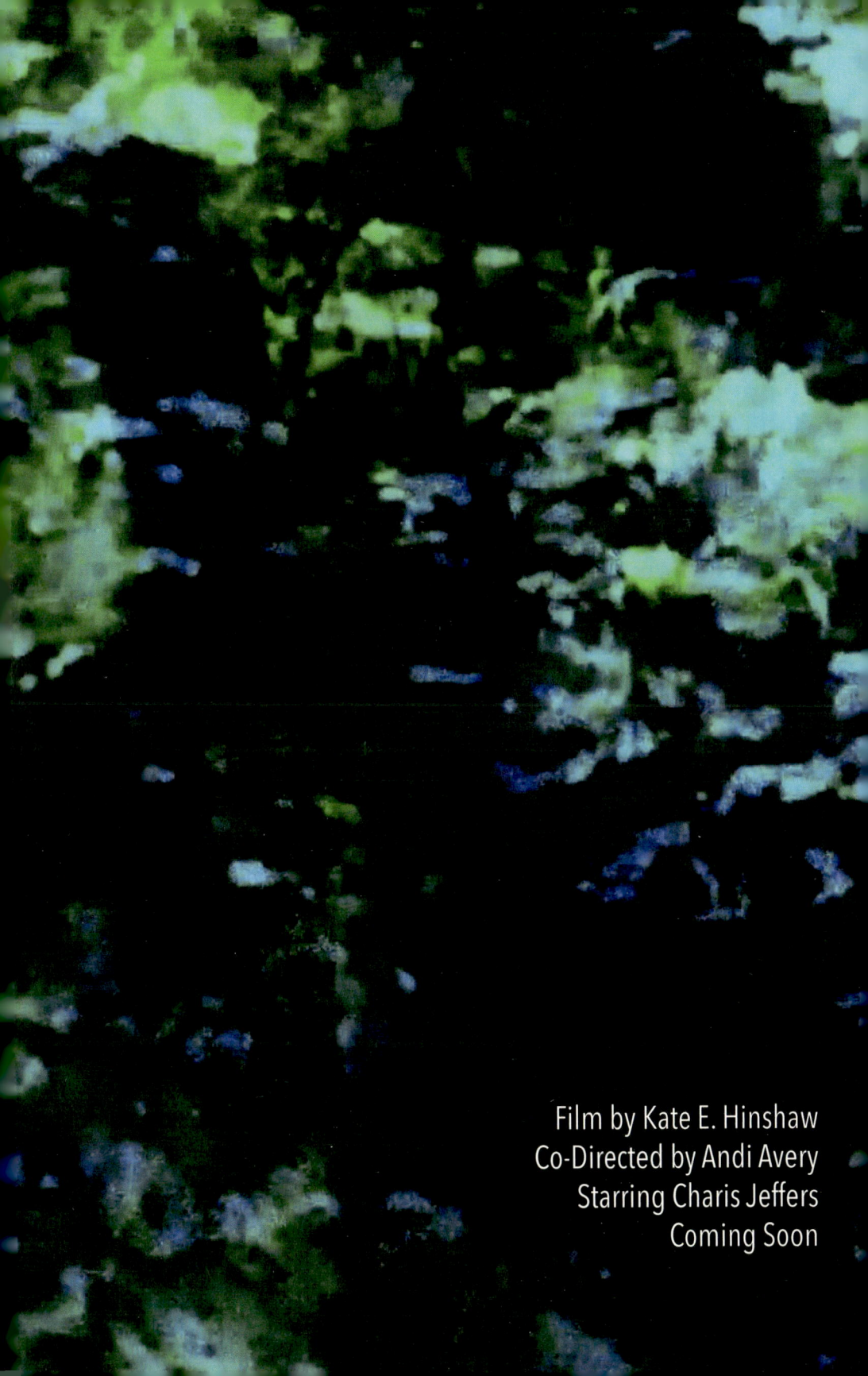

Film by Kate E. Hinshaw
Co-Directed by Andi Avery
Starring Charis Jeffers
Coming Soon

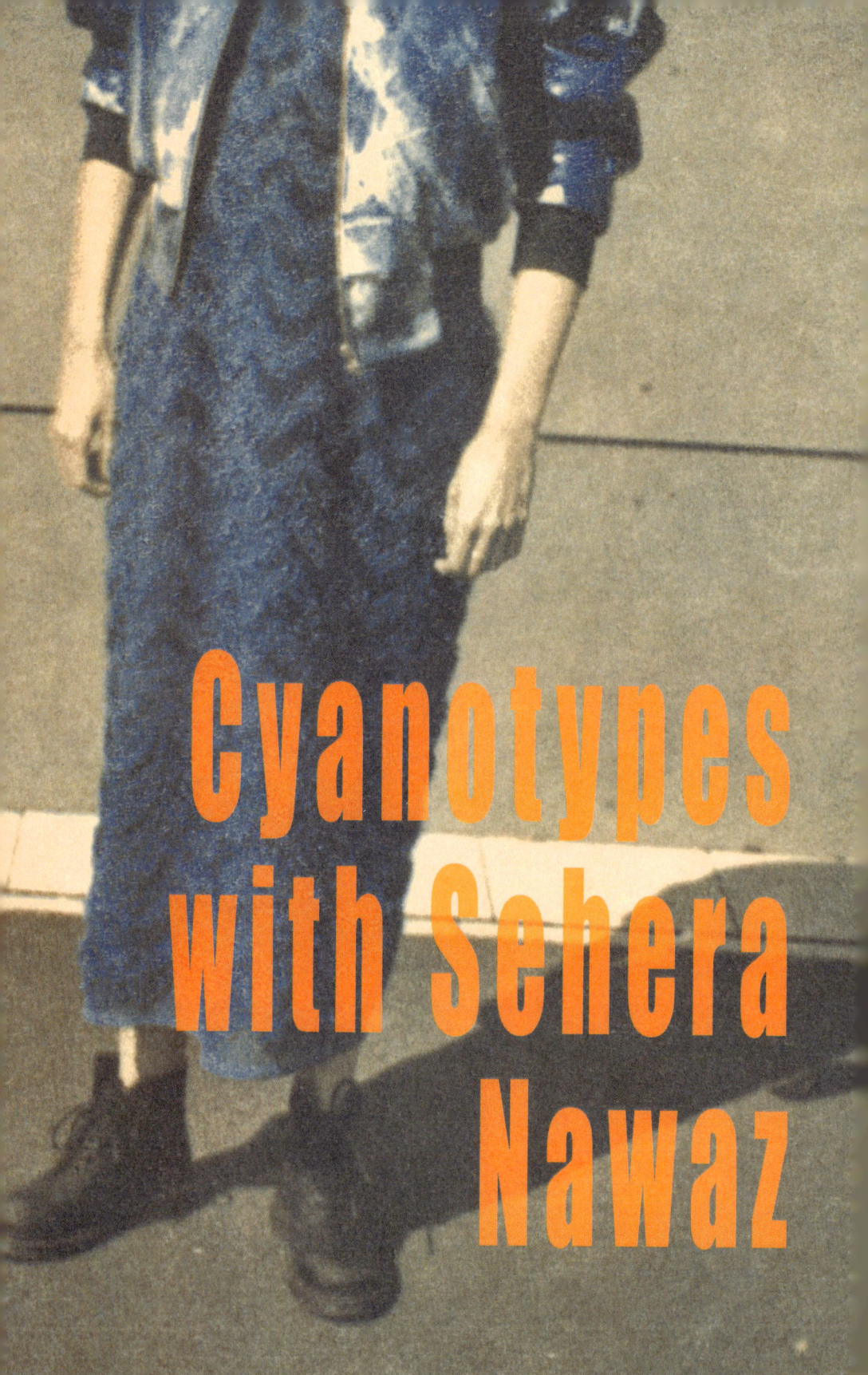

Cyanotypes with Sehera Nawaz

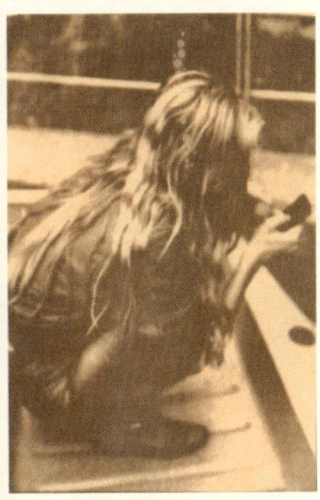
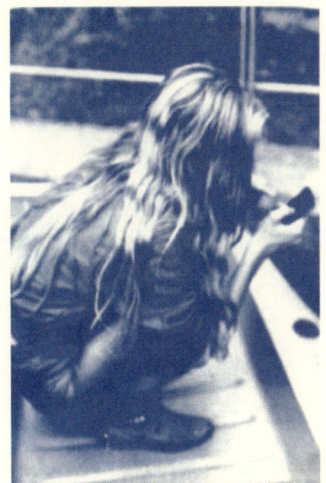
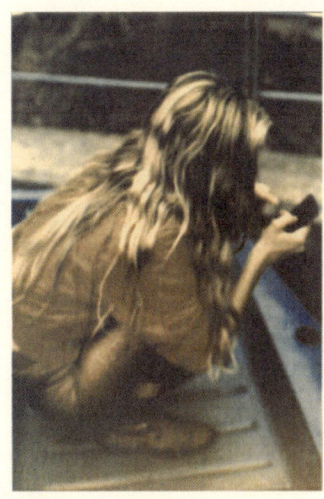

Tell us about yourself.

I am a Berlin based, passionate analog and alternative photographer specialized in cyanotypes. In my artistic practice I thoroughly study analog photography techniques that inspire me due to their limited controllability. I push these techniques to their limits by experimenting with different materials as support or creating new ways of exposing and coloring them. The divide of old techniques seen with new eyes is source for my inspiration.

You have a background in computer science and now work with old photographic printing techniques. How did these two worlds collide?

Early in my studies I specialized on 3D rendering technologies and later worked for some years in that field. For people who don't know, rendering in the digital film business is the part where you actually calculate the lighting of a shot and produce an image out of the 0 and 1s that define the 3D scene. Basically it is the camera of the whole system. I was lucky enough to be part of an excellent team of coders who created the new renderer for a big film company in New Zealand. Unfortunately I was missing home and friends, so when I decided to come back I was lost as to what I could do next. I was also fed up with sitting in front of the computer for 50 hours a week. When I found analog photography it dawned on me, that all the knowledge about the behavior of light is really helping me understand these old techniques and actually make it possible for me to push them even further and invent or research new processes. My passion became my new calling.

Tell us about your dark room process. How do you deal with remjet when processing C41?

Well, as I use photography film I don't have to deal with remjet. :) I have a studio in the basement of a collective in Berlin, where I process my film and where I create the negatives for the two colored cyanotype process. A lot of it is choosing the right image for the process, as using only two colors can only work well if these two colors are actually present in the image. I am still working out a way to make the process fully analog, as I have to split the color negative into two black and white negatives that represent the image well. Up untill now I have been doing that by scanning the color negatives, splitting them and reprinting them as black and white negatives for contact printing. The cyanotype process is said to be one of the easiest to learn, but it is also hard to get a reliable good result. The two colored cyanotype process has two layers of print on top of each other. You coat a piece of paper with the prepared emulsion and after contact printing the first layer, it is a deep Prussian Blue. Now you put it in fresh black tea (not too hot, otherwise you usually damage the paper), leave it there for about 10 min or more (no need to be precise, I also left it over night and it worked very well). After toning you "bleach" it with washing soda, to remove any trace of remaining Prussian Blue. When the print is dry, you are ready for the second coating. Now you use the negative for the blue parts of the image, you just

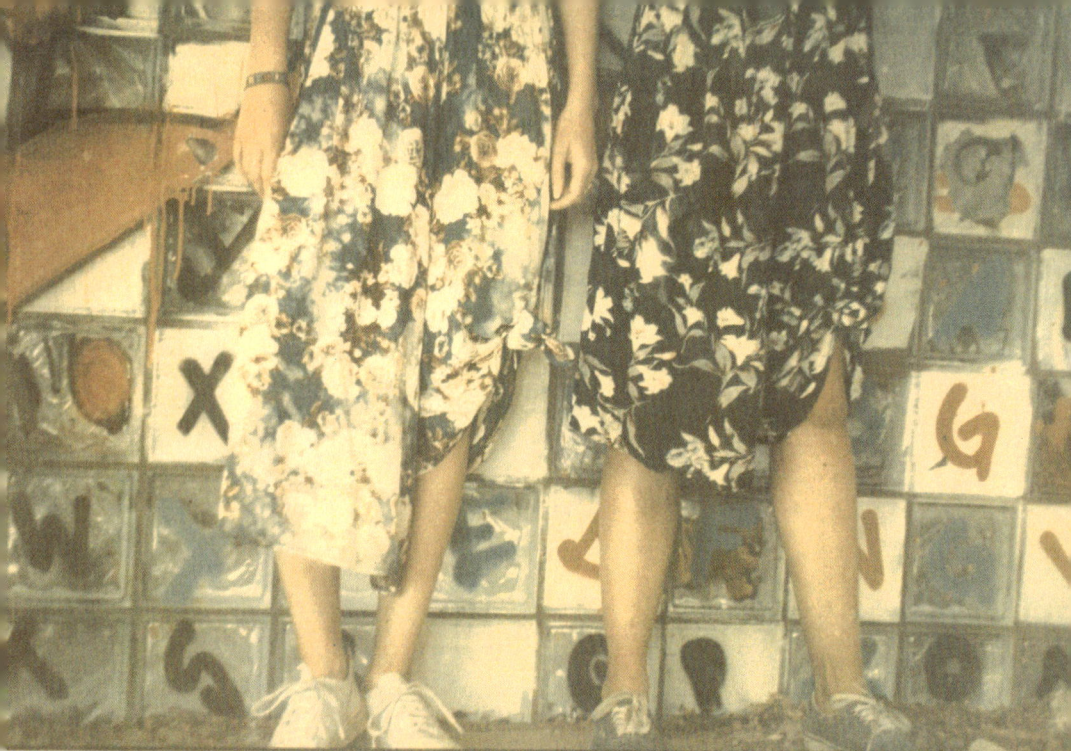

have to place it very precisely directly onto the first print. Develop with water as usually and done!

How did you come up with the idea of incorporating black tea into your cyanotypes?

It is amazing how so many people know the cyanotype process, but have not seen the wide range of colors that can be produced by toning with tea or coffee or other things with tannin. It is actually a very well documented way of changing the blue. But it took a lot of searching to find the right tea to get this reddish color, as mostly it turns brownish with black tea.

Why film? What attracts you to working with celluloid?

When I was still working for the film company I learned to look very closely at images, to find the flaws of the rendering process. You look for patterns in pixels and noise, or lack thereof. It was always the goal, not to see any patterns in shadows or depth of field blur. The noise produced by analog photography is very pleasing to the eye, so that was the first thing that drew me to analog. What kept me there is the fact, that you work with your hands and most importantly, that you cannot control everything. People usually strive for more control, but I deeply feel that in order to understand this ever changing world, we need to give up on control and that we can only truly master a technique if we

can let go. Especially the two colored process can not be controlled fully and I love the element of randomness, that one could call 'life'. You can strive for more control, but even using a fresh batch of tea every time does not guarantee you the same result in toning. And we are not even talking about the fact that you will not be able to coat a paper the same way every time.

Do you have a favorite film stock?

I actually love to use expired slide film and cross process it. It has the grain of a slide film and usually looks like it has a pink filter over everything. So AGFA Precisa CT100 slide film or Fujichrome Provia 100F. For something less experimental I love KODAK Protra 400/800. B&W I usually use Illford FP4, it is reliable to develop in caffenol and easy to push and pull.

You teach cyanotype classes in Berlin. What do you want students to walk away with after taking a class with you?

The student should walk away with a feeling of how easy it is to produce something beautiful with their hands. But also, I love giving them a sneak peek into the depth of the process. Usually they go home with a bunch of artwork they created in a few hours of fun.

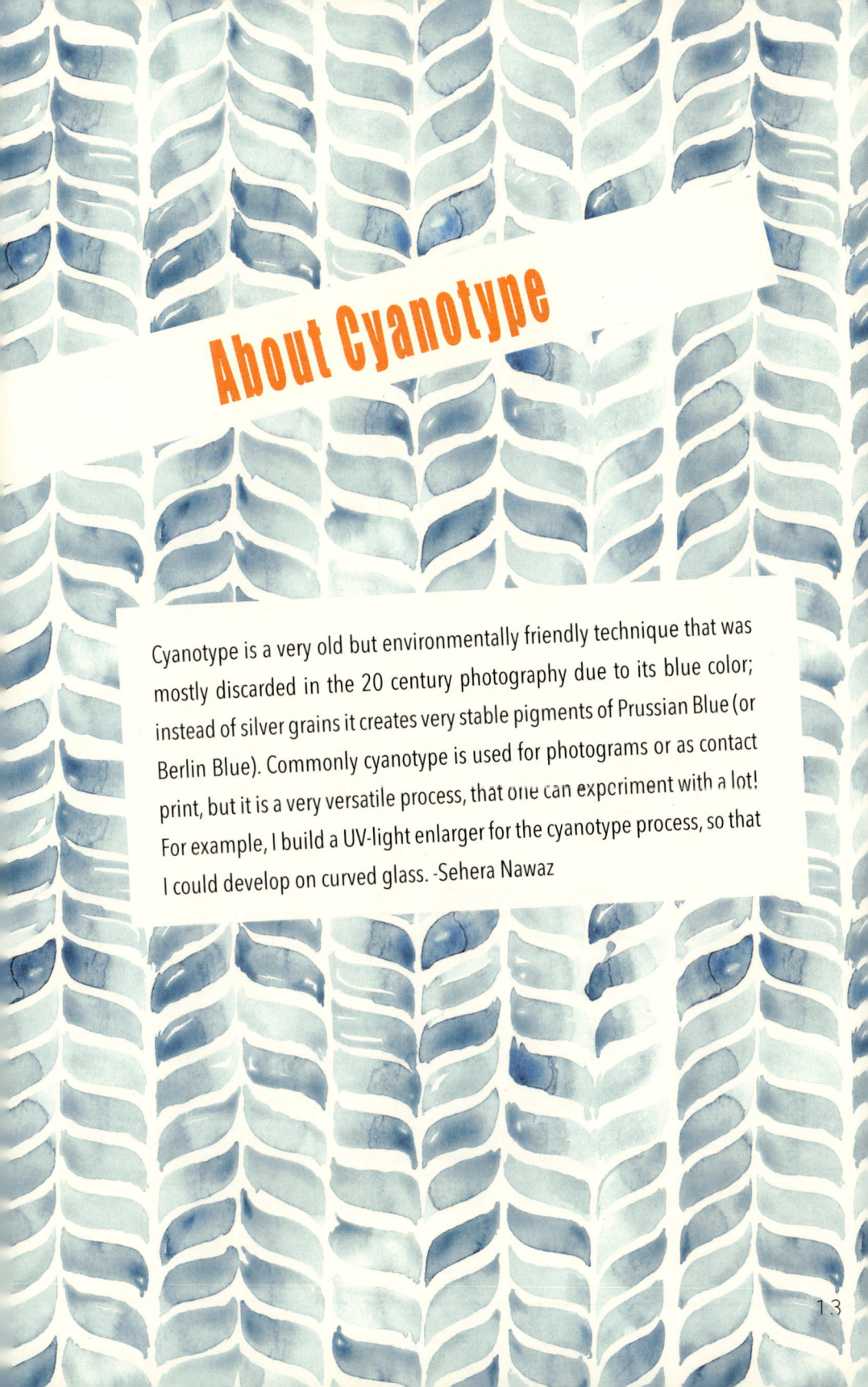

About Cyanotype

Cyanotype is a very old but environmentally friendly technique that was mostly discarded in the 20 century photography due to its blue color; instead of silver grains it creates very stable pigments of Prussian Blue (or Berlin Blue). Commonly cyanotype is used for photograms or as contact print, but it is a very versatile process, that one can exprciment with a lot! For example, I build a UV-light enlarger for the cyanotype process, so that I could develop on curved glass. -Sehera Nawaz

Sister Portal

Maleny, Queensland, Australia.

I'm walking in an overgrown paddock, a patch of cleared rainforest my Father has convinced his partner to buy. My ten pound navy desert boots from Spitalfields make sense in this context. Recently returned from two years in London, I can see more clearly than usual the green vibrations of this place. I'm thirty three years old and accompanied by my half brothers, Rory, five and Sacha three, we are headed to the creek that is the back boundary. Dad has slashed the grass in an effort to clear up a rubbish dump from the previous owners. Rory announces that there is treasure in the paddock, and right on cue I see a roll of 8mm film in the leaf litter.

Before leaving the UK I attended an analog film workshop in Bethnal Green. I learned about the artists who would leave their film in raw meat, rubbish or even bury it in the ground just to see the effect of the bacteria on the film surface when projected. Excited, I try to explain to the little boys that there are images trapped on the black circle in my hand. They want to see this for themselves before they'll believe it.

Toowoomba, Queensland, Australia.

Back at my Mum's, the house my brother and I grew up in, I retrieve from my packed up belongings the Agfa Family film viewer an ex-girlfriend had salvaged for me from The Brotherhood of St Lawrence charity bins in Melbourne years before. My childhood bedroom is still the best place to experiment with something tricky and interesting. The luminous green of the image shocks me. It jerks and slips as I pull the brittle film past the light. Few times before or since have I felt the magic of that moment. I wish Rory and Sacha were with me to see that what I had told them was true. It's unsettling to want to share a moment with siblings three decades younger than myself.

I am actually aghast when the silhouette of a boy's head and neck makes itself known from behind the mottled green. Fumbling to operate the mechanism of the foreign machine I manage to make it play.

I've read enough Maya Deren to know that film can be a time machine. I'm enough of a mystic to believe in portals and messages from other places.

The roll of film was shot off all in one go. The backyard swimming pool remains in the shot as the two boys skylark for the camera. They jump in and out of the water, flash their towels and taunt the person behind the camera. There is only one other image at the end of the roll, a woman sunbathing on a banana lounge.

There in my bedroom with the Agfa Family, I phone my friend Joseph and try to explain the epiphany of the moment. It was like a moment in a Tim Winton novel, only on film. The motion, texture, and color of the bacteria seem purely Australian to me. Nature had created its own mise-en-scene to convey something visceral. Of course he can't understand.

Years prior I had success painting film and knew where to send the dirty roll to have it transferred. The imagery lost some of it's luminescence but when I matched it to a demo track of a friend's song it was haunting and Australian and affective.

Seven years later it's still hard to write about this film and how I found it. No one I've shown it to has ever seemed to understand its magic. People are put off by the steady voyeurism of the gaze, and the nudity of the children. A close friend even suggested I should clean off the mould so she could see the children properly. My brother Jock from my parents' marriage came closest when he classed it as biodegradable and from another plane. He said there would be no way I could screen it in this world at this time. I felt he was probably right.

Skye Thompson

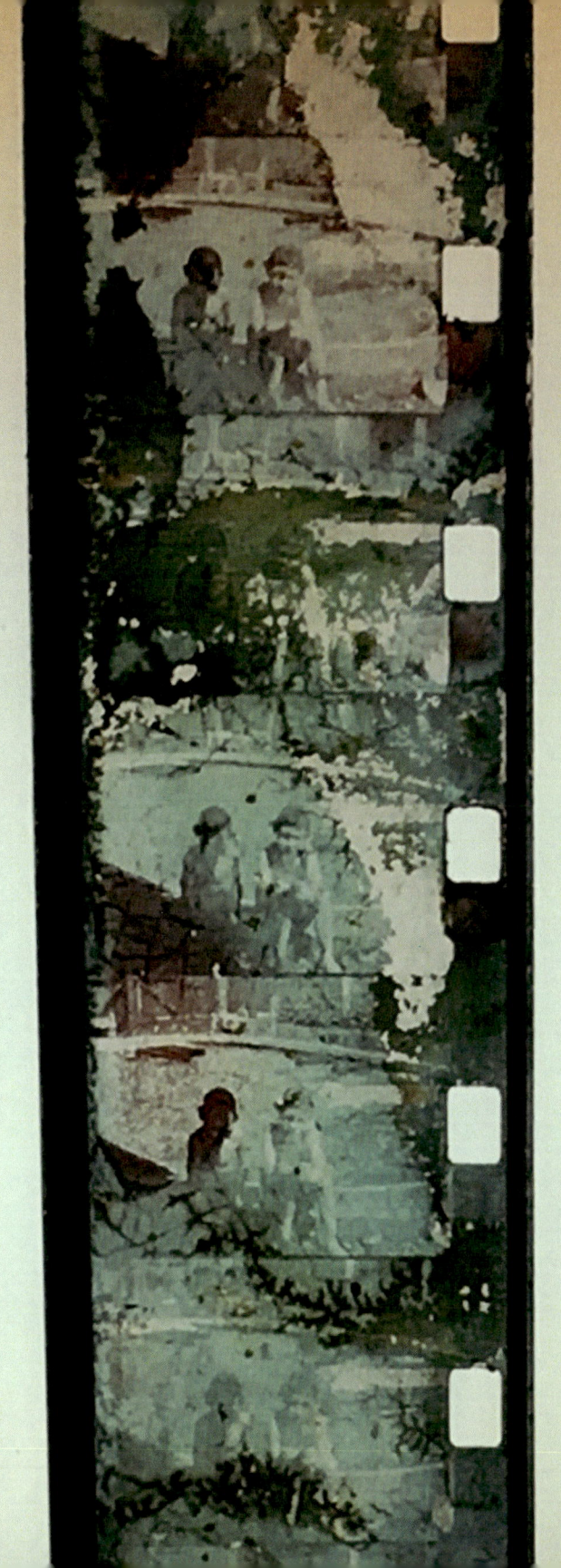

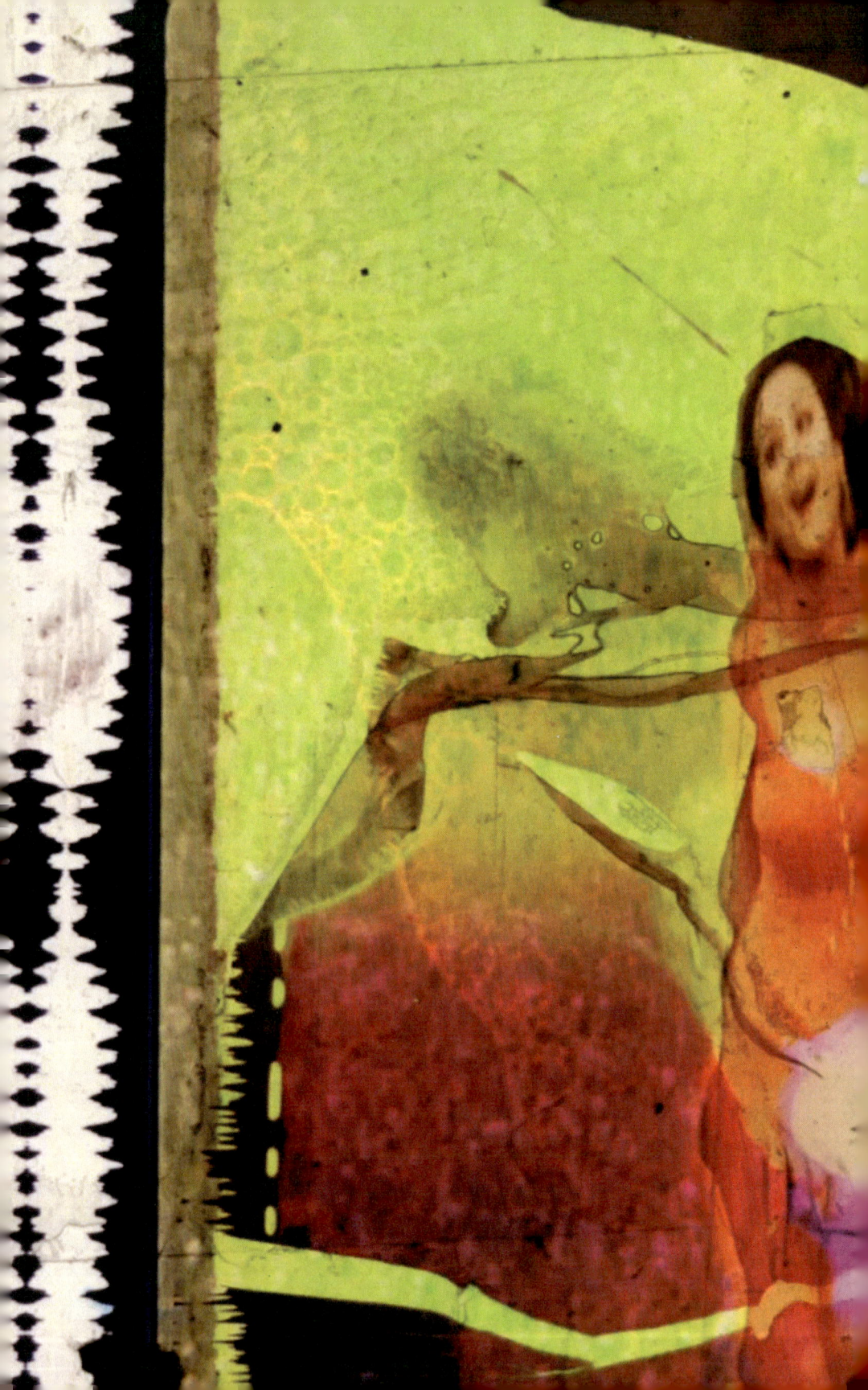

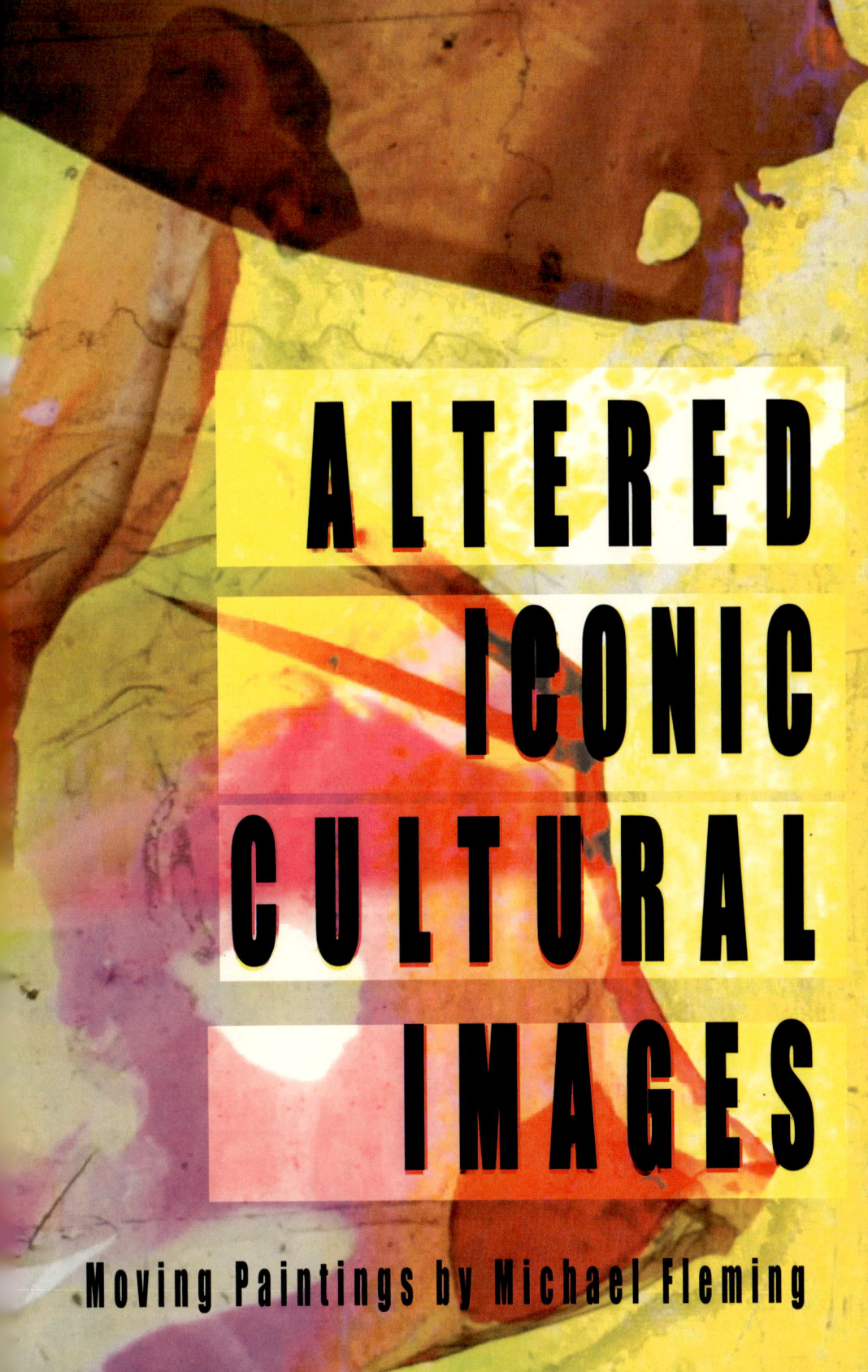

ALTERED ICONIC CULTURAL IMAGES

Moving Paintings by Michael Fleming

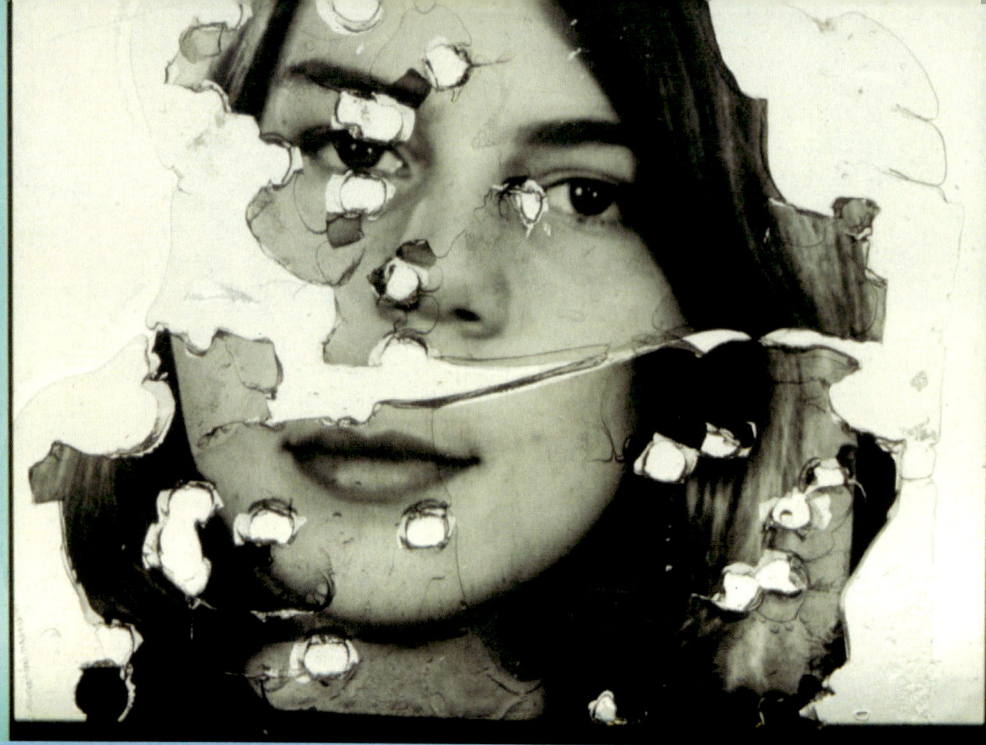

In *Never Never Land* and *The Garden of Delight*, you're actively challenging perfectionism and the idea of paradise by disrupting the frame. Can you describe your process with these films?

The Garden of Delight (2017) started as a reaction on a previous film *Over&Over* (2015) that was mainly about violence. I wanted to do the opposite, to make a film about love and romance. So I started to collect a lot of romantic films, taking out the useful parts, and taping them together. Like a patchwork, it slowly expands. I let the images dictate direction and let it all happen and react by free association and intuition. Themes like kissing, being happy together, and getting undressed came to the surface, but it didn't get any further than a cliché. Later I came across a reproduction of the triptych *The Garden of delight* by Jeronimus Bosch that helped define the structure of the film. I studied the painting closely. The more I went into it the more it became clear that this painting had themes that I wanted to explore in my film--paradise, lust, and hell. I used imagery of fruit, birds, butterflies, lovers, sex, porn, demons, and fire. That is the beauty of found footage. It guides you and takes you by the hand. The process of making the film and the subject of the painting became the content. Both are about chance, transformation, and how beauty can shift to cruelty, from heaven to hell

and the vice versa.

With the film *Never Never Land* (2018), I wanted to go further with the knife cutting I used in my film *The Garden of Delight*. I had this idea to use the film as skin. I started to collect film commercials about skin and beauty care, medical nursing slides, and dental x-rays from my dentist. I read Dr. Frankenstein and books about gene editing, plastic surgery, etc. I was collecting as many subject matters and possibilities. Literary and figurative sewing, sticking, gluing them together and cutting them apart to make it a totality. *Never Never Land* dissects our obsession with physical perfection and desire for control. Chance is replaced by choice and a belief in infinite possibility through engineering our lives and bodies as the ultimate DIY project in search of Homo Perfectus.

In *Over&Over* you use film frames from major Hollywood films to discuss fear of mortality. What inspired this film?

In *Over&Over* there was no plan, no script, or scenario. It started with a hunch, a small idea. It was just simply guns. I wanted to pull the trigger and start shooting. Wouldn't it be cool to have a movie where from the first second the shooting starts? There are a lot of guns in cinema trailers. So I started to collect trailers, take out the useful parts, and tape them together. Like a patchwork it slowly expanded and got bigger.

I discovered themes and subjects--one handed shooters, double handed shooters, machine guns, screaming shooters, bazookas, and explosions. Slowly chapters revealed themselvs--suspense, fear, shootings, car chase, explosions, and voila! There was the beginning of a new film. It's a long slow process. You have a lot of time to think about what you're looking at and study the subject. Almost every film trailer has the same story. A happy family, couple, or group is attacked or violated and responds with revenge. The same story is been told over and over again--like a recipe, formula, or commercial. Fear and revenge is a product--you can shape your own life, stop being an innocent victim and become a co-conspirator.

What's your favorite tool to use when physically altering celluloid?

There are so many. The fun thing is that each film has its own subject and character whic asks for its own solution and approach. For example in *Never Never Land* form and content are intertwined.

The editing becomes surgery and the film material itself becomes a metaphor for skin. Also using a knife, a sewing machine, glue and tape to combine different film material together has a literal and figuratively purpose and meaning. In *Over &Over* I also wanted to accentuate the subject of destruction to burn the film image and the film material itself.

By stripping and scalping the filmic images and showing the optical sound waveform next to the sprocket holes I want to emphasize the fact that we are not only looking at images but also looking at the film material itself, which kills the image so to speak.

The new film I am working on now is about birth and death. It is linear with a beginning and an end, which suits the subject perfectly. In this film I'm experimenting with celluloid approaches like film-decay, using my own old home movies from my youth, digging in memory, time, and decline. For me experimental film is the perfect pool to dive into the unknown, to let it all happen, react, and encounter the images intuitively by using a painterly approach from my pictorial roots.

You've screened your work all over! Do you have a favorite festival you've screened at?

Participating in a film festival is a real joy. The nice festivals are like a giant jacuzzi, bubbling in it for days, meeting inspiring filmmakers, and seeing new films. There are so many. Each fest has its own character, style, and potential. Some are great for meeting fellow filmmakers, others are good in participating with the audience, some are located in a beautiful town, and some have great parties. I enjoyed Ann Arbor Film Festival, Chicago Underground Film Festival, Lausanne Underground Film and Music Festival, Curto Circuito in Santiago de Compostela, Fracto Berlin, Alchemy Hawick, Analogica in Italy and many more. Of course it is a nice when a festival compensates travel costs.

Your films are so visceral. They cut deep. What do you want your audience to walk away feeling?

I hope people can dive into the same adventure I'm experiencing while making a movie and discover the conceptual connections, associations, and juxtapositions, not only by looking at the film cognitively and aesthetically but also by having physical involvement.

What's next for you, anything else to add?

I have been experimenting with Duraclear film-large transparent photos for light-boxes. It is similar to 35mm analog film only a bit bigger. I will continue to work more with these film still transparent images.

Lately I've been doing workshops on film manipulation techniques and how to collage on film material. The objective of these workshops is to explore and practice ideas around camera-less filmmaking and work directly with found footage. We analyze the footage, study the physical approach, dismantle the film, lift the emulsion layer, and work with simple household chemicals and a knife to cut into the film. My films couldn't been made without the cooperation of Aaron Michael Smith and Onno Peterson. Aaron Michael Smith (Boston, USA) is the composer of most of my films. We met at the Chicago Underground film festival. It is a pleasure to work with such a talented musician. His music reveals another unknown layer brought to the surface. The digitalization is made by Onno Peterson (Amsterdam, Netherlands). He is the man who makes it possible to transfers my analog 35mm films to a digital file. He developed his own frame by frame machine to do this.

Herbal Developers
General Treegan

Photo developed with hibiscus developer

This project was generously supported by the chemistry team and developing technicians at the laboratories of Churubusco. It is one of the LEC [Experimental Film Lab Mexico] and Churubusco Studios and Film Labs residency program 2018.

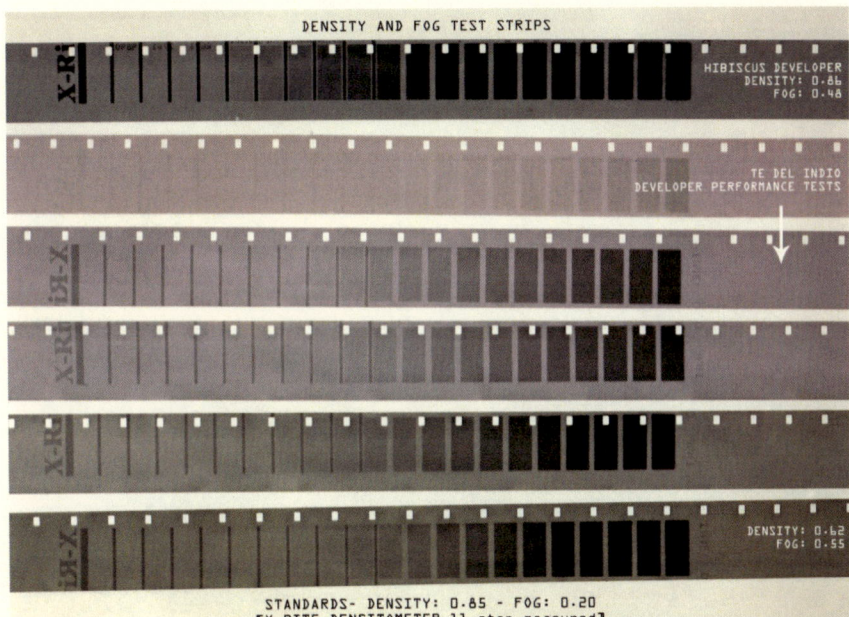

Herbalism is botany applied to medicine. It comprises of the extractive use of medicinal plants or their derivatives for therapeutic purposes, often for the prevention or treatment of pathologies. Herbalism holds a strong presence in traditional cultures of Mexican medicine.

The outright objective of my residency project was to formulate B&W motion picture film developers based on Mexican plants used in traditional medicine, attempt to standardize their preparation method, and to process film with them. One way to contibute to the long term sustainability of home-processing of film is to further research into safer and simpler non-commercial developer processes.

Why Herbalism?

Plant-based developers have been used for many years. The idea of formulating a developer based on Yerba Mate [Ilex Paraguaiensis], a typical drink where I am originally from in South American, came to me via an article about Phil Hoffman's Film Farm. The developer not only worked perfectly, but was also economical, could be reused, and was eco-friendly.

The base developing formula used was that of Caffenol CM. Caffenol is currently the most famous and frequently used eco-friendly developer.

Upon invitation by the LEC to be part of the LEC-CHURUBUSCO residencies, I was immediately struck by the idea to use plants, specifically, those used in the traditional medicine of indigenous Mexicans, to achieve the formulation of a 100% Mexican photographic developer.

The project included close and fundamental collaboration with the chemistry team at the laboratories of Churubusco Studios, achieving an interchange between science, experimentation, and art, to achieve the results outlined below. We tested these developers for stability, pH and range, and resulting density, to evaluate their effectiveness. In general, all developers have pH above 10, a level which denotes an energetic developer.

Preparation of an Herbal Developer

Most plants contain tannins that by hydrolysis it form an acid and a base. In general, this acid is phenolic or gallic. Both can reduce the silver present in photographic film so that it is feasible to formulate a developer from them. Three extraction methods were used:

+ Boiling the plant source in water for 30 minutes.
+ Steeping the plant in hot water for a day.
+ Steeping the plant in hot water and alcohol for a day.

The differences across results of these three methods were impreceptible, so it was decided to steep the plants in hot water for a day, as that was the easiest method to carry out.

The method is simple. The dry leaf of the plant is placed in a glass or plastic jar that can tolerate hot water. Add 650 ml of boiling water, and leave for one day. Then, filter the liquid (with a paper or cloth filter) to remove the rough tea and plant leaves, sticks, etc. The resulting amount of liquid should be around 500 ml.

The tea-infusion can be placed in a refrigerator for use in the following days, or you can even freeze the liquid for use in later months if you are using season flowers.

For each 100 ml of resulting tea/infusion, add 8 grams of sodium carbonate and 2 grams of ascorbic acid. Some leaves absorb more water than others, so the resulting liquid may be less than 500 ml In these cases, add boiling water to top-up to the 500 ml mark.

21

HIBISCUS DEVELOPER

To prepare the tea/infusion, use 50 grams of Hibiscus flower in 650 ml ofwater.

Tea	500ml of hibiscus tea
Sodium CArbonate	40g
Ascorbic Acid	10g
Kbr [potassium bromide]	0.5 g [optional]

TÉ DEL INDIO DEVELOPER [Mexican Indian Tea]

To prepare the tea/infusion, use 40 grams of mixed leaves in 650 ml ofwater.

Tea	500ml of "Té del Indio" tea
Sodium CArbonate	40g
Ascorbic Acid	10g
Kbr [potassium bromide]	0.5 g [optional]

ARNICA DEVELOPER

To prepare the tea/infusion, use 20 grams of Arnica flowers and leaves in 650 ml ofwater.

Tea	500ml of Arnica tea
Sodium CArbonate	40g
Ascorbic Acid	10g
Kbr [potassium bromide]	0.5 g [optional]

All tests used Kodak 5302, Kodak 3378, and ORWO UP21, processed as a negative. The resulting chemical fog is tolerable if the negative is transferred via telecine or scanning. If using the negative for contact printing it is recommended to employ the potassium bromide option suggested, above.

These formulas employed a standard developer time of 12 minutes at 26ºC for all films tested in the first use, the good thing is that it could be reused. If using another film stock, development times can be obtained through comparison with other developers or through some tests.

First developer use: 12 min@ 26ºC
Second use: 16min@ 26ºC
Third use: 22min @ 26ºC
Fourth use: 30min @ 30ºC

Herbalist developers verify the power of traditional plants, demonstrating the rich cultural heritage of the indigenous peoples of what is now Mexico.
To the right is a study of the gamma and density curves of a test strip developed with Hibiscus tea, as well as the evolution of tests with "Té del Indio." Compared to a standard cinematographic laboratory curve, these test results demonstrate strikingly similar tonal ranges and density. Hibiscus tea results do demonstrate a greater chemical fog, which is evident in the lower region of the curve.

SENSITOMETRY CURVE

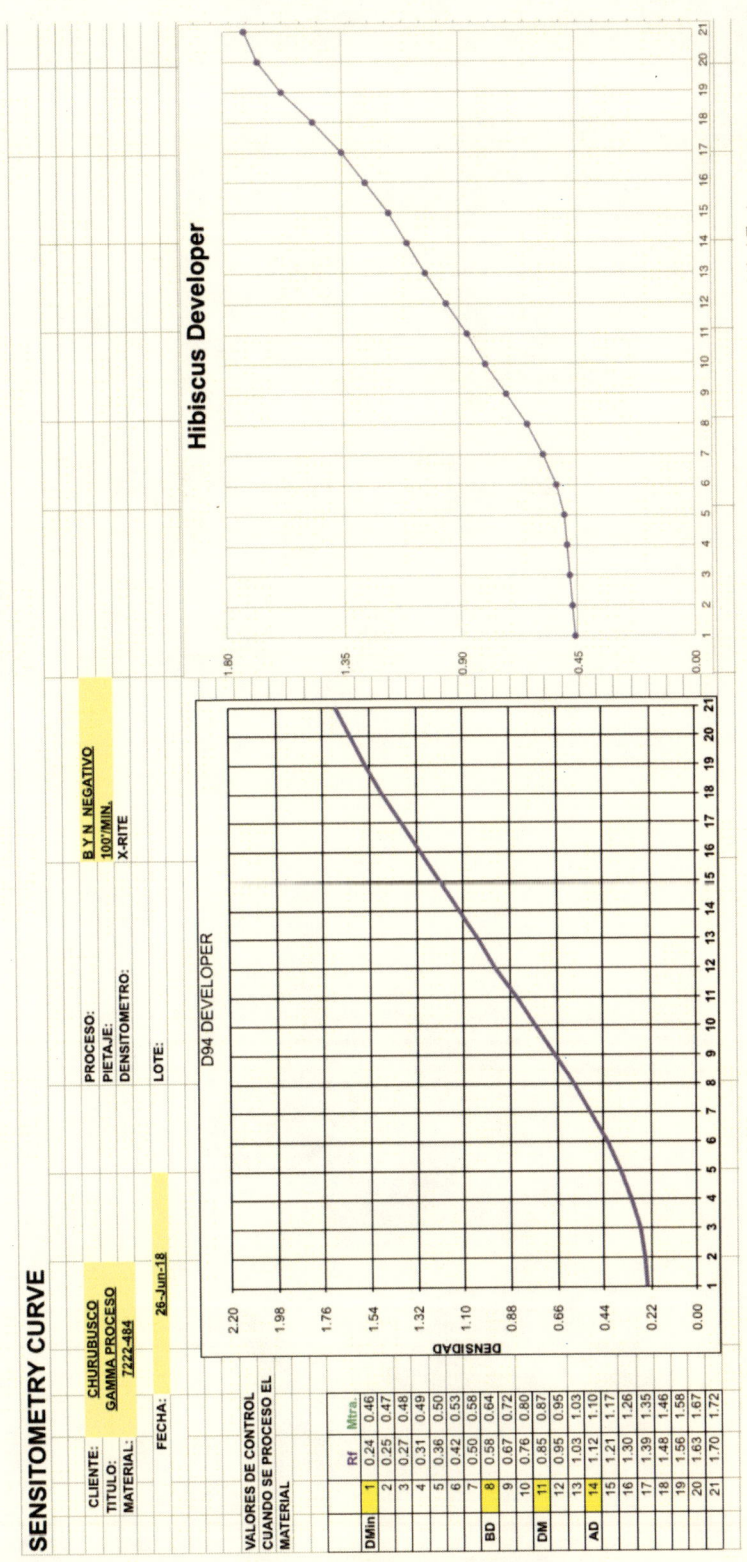

CLIENTE: CHURUBUSCO
TITULO: GAMMA PROCESO
MATERIAL: 7222-484

FECHA: 26-Jun-18

PROCESO: B Y N NEGATIVO
PIETAJE: 100'/MIN.
DENSITOMETRO: X-RITE

LOTE:

Hibiscus Developer

D94 DEVELOPER

DENSIDAD

VALORES DE CONTROL
CUANDO SE PROCESO EL
MATERIAL

		Rf	Mtra.
DMin	1	0.24	0.46
	2	0.25	0.47
	3	0.27	0.48
	4	0.31	0.49
	5	0.36	0.50
	6	0.42	0.53
	7	0.50	0.58
BD	8	0.58	0.64
	9	0.67	0.72
	10	0.76	0.80
DM	11	0.85	0.87
	12	0.95	0.95
	13	1.03	1.03
AD	14	1.12	1.10
	15	1.21	1.17
	16	1.30	1.26
	17	1.39	1.35
	18	1.48	1.46
	19	1.56	1.58
	20	1.63	1.67
	21	1.70	1.72

23

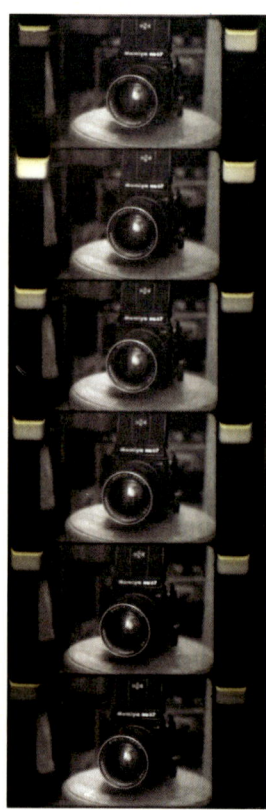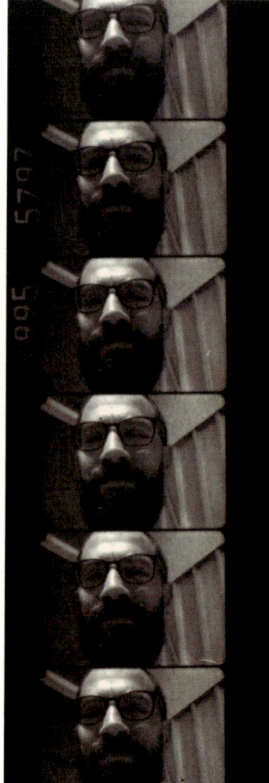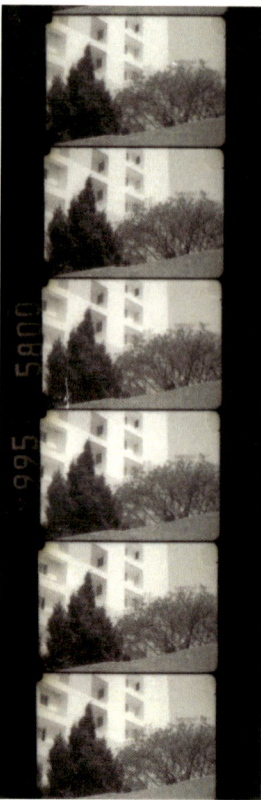

Té del Indio Developer

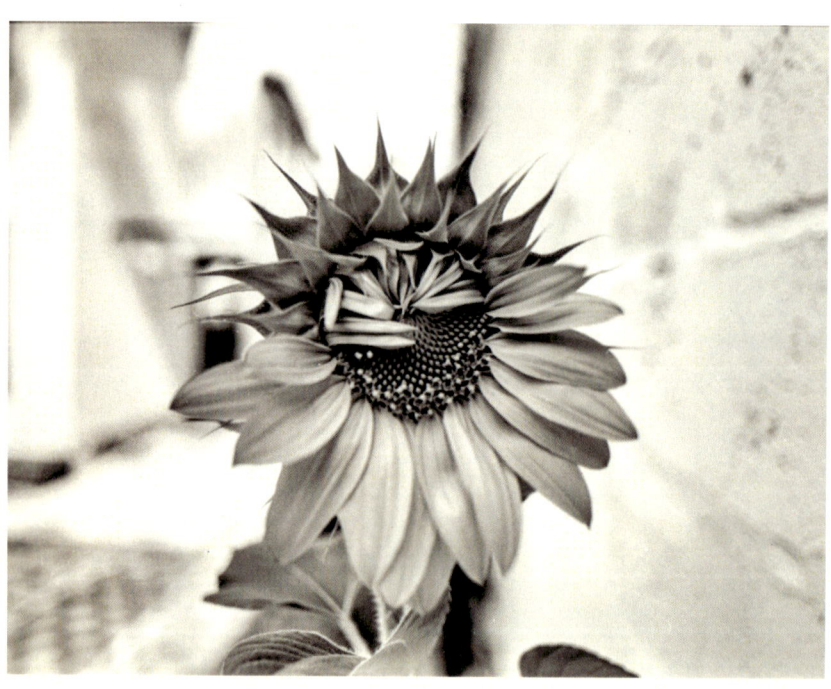

Arnica Developer

CALL FOR SUBMISSION
Let's be a forest - a collective film project

At the symposium "Film in the present tense" in Berlin, Germany in October 2017 Mark Toscano showed a film he shot just a few days earlier in LA (16mm, b/w reversal).
After his presentation he cut the film into pieces and gave it to the audience. I got 18 frames of a palm tree and I remember that during his presentation he said "you cannot have LA without palm trees".

Since so many analog filmmakers from around the world attended this symposium I thought: You cannot have an analog film community without filmmakers.
We are so many great filmmakers from around the world and we are really good connected... so why not make a film together? Let's be a forest!

I am asking you to send me an already processed piece of 16mm film showing a tree. It is completely your decision what kind of tree or what kind of film you are sending to me. Also it will be your decision how long the piece of film is.

I will collect the filmstrips and will edit them to one film, letting the different film strips become one work, letting single trees become one united forest.
Note: I might make them shorter, depending on what the final film needs.

There is no deadline for this project. The forest should grow endlessly.
However, as I would like to give the film the possibility to be screened, there will be different editions. (e.g. Let's be a forest – Autumn 2019 edition)

Filmmakers, who already contributed (in order of receiving the film strips):
Mark Toscano, Debora S. Philips, Alex Mackenzie, Anna Petruzelová, Karel Doing, Manfred Schwaba, Peter Humble, Gaëlle Rouard, Douglas Urbank, Andrei Florin, Thomas Chatard.

Looking forward to your contribution. The more the merrier.

Please send 16mm film showing a tree to:
Stefanie Weberhofer
Geusaugasse 15/10
1030 Wien (Vienna)
AUSTRIA, EUROPE

You can also reach out to me via email in advance, if you want: mail@stayfanny.com

Stefanie Weberhofer

Doing the Reel Thing

Today the use of analog film material is not essential anymore, as people can capture their important moments easily with their smart phones, or if they are very ambitious and prefer a more cinematic look, they shoot on their DSLRs. The film industry too is not very much interested in the use of film stock anymore. It seems that digital technology is the new and therefore better thing and is on its best way to replace this out-dated and obsolete way of producing movies. Professional film labs are shutting down, one after the other, as they run out of business. The case here seems very clear: The glorious times of analog filmmaking are over and movies have arrived in the digital era. Or is it possible that analog filmmaking is still a thing? Is it maybe the 'reel' thing? In this essay I'll discuss the art of independent, analog filmmaking in the digital era and the rise of artist-run film labs in the last decade.

What I mean with the term independent analog filmmaking is simply the act of working with film material autonomously without the dependence of a commercial film production company which supports or influences the project in any way. This form of working on Super 8, 16mm, or 35mm film is usually used in the realm of experimental or avant-garde film. To have more artistic choices and the full control of the film material, from the moment when the filmmakers put the film into the camera to the final projection of it, the independent analog filmmakers usually also refuse to work with the help of commercial film laboratories. The filmmakers hand-process the film on their own, sometimes in a kitchen sink, sometimes in a bath tub, but always independent. As filmmaking (especially analog filmmaking) requires a lot of equipment like cameras, editing tables, and projectors to name only the most important devices, it can get very expensive when you have to buy and store that all on

your own. This is one of the main reasons why artist-run film labs were formed. The first one was created in 1966, *The London Filmmakers' Cooperative*. "A cinema lab run by the filmmakers themselves, as poorly equipped as they were in the beginning, was established." A few more labs emerged in the following years mostly in Europe. It was not until the 1990s that the idea of creating an independent film lab became more popular.

In 1990, three students from the Arnhem School of Art in the Netherlands refused to accept that their school had gotten rid of film equipment to buy video equipment. They wanted to film on Super 8. They rescued the machines from a lab which had just shut down and started up *Studio Een*. In 1992 some students from Braunschweig created *Sector 16* in Hanover. This period proved to be a point of departure for a whole group of structures in Europe.

In 2010 when digital high-end cameras like ARRI Alexa were introduced to the market and allowed a complete digital workflow for creating mainstream movies the industry's use of film material changed extremely. Only two years later almost all cinemas replaced their 35mm projectors with new digital ones. The Austrian analog filmmaker and purist Peter Kubelka described the year 2012 as the saddest year in film history as film was no longer a part of cinema anymore. The use of film material is no longer essential for the industry, that fact changed the industry completely. This shift in the industry resulted in a rise of independent artist-run film labs.

The decline in commercial film production, however, has been countered by a rebirth in the phenomenon of artist-run film laboratories. What in the early Nineties was limited to a handful of cooperatively owned, independent labs, mostly in France, has grown into an international network of over 30, many of them formed within the last

27

several years.

The decline of using actual film material for professional productions led to a left-over of unwanted and mostly cheap equipment which in the right hands could be used for smaller-scale and independent operations in artist-run labs. "Saved from the scrap heap, many discarded contact printers and lomo processing tanks have begun a second life as artists' tools." When Ed Lachman, the cinematographer of Todd Haynes film *Carol*, found out that the laboratory Technicolor in New York City would close after processing *Carol* last film he could not believe it.

"I went and asked them what was going to become of all the equipment, the continuous processors… I was told that everything would most likely be tossed in the dumpster, simply because nobody wanted any of it. Can you imagine that, dragging an entire continuous processing and printing rig to the dump, some $250,000 worth of equipment, at least! That really made me feel awful. I called my key grip and I asked him if he had a bit of room in the warehouse where he keeps his gear… We picked up the whole lot of it, and as a result, I am now the owner of a dismantled photochemical laboratory."

Most artist-run film labs are located in Europe, there is LaborBerlin in Germany, filmkoop wien in Austria, no.w.here in London, UK and L'Abominable in Paris, France to name just a few. But the trend is also coming to North America. There are the Double Negatives in Montreal, LIFT in Toronto and Mono no Aware in New York City. All of these initiatives offer the opportunity for DIY analog filmmaking with darkrooms and equipment. In order to share this almost forgotten knowledge most of them offer workshops for beginners too. Through the websites filmlabs.org and frameworks.org filmmakers have the chance to be connected with each other. It is a network, organized to help and support each other.

But what is it that makes this form of filmmaking and artist-run film labs so cool? Well, first of all there is the element of passion that the filmmaker requires to work in this way. I would say passion is the essential ingredient for creating *reel* films, as the artists work very close with their material for a very long time. The filmmakers touch the film material with their hands when they open the package and put the film into the camera, when they process it, when they edit it and when they project it. When the material gets exposed to light the chemical emulsion changes, in the developing process it turns either translucent or opaque and when finally the light of the projector goes through the material and generates an image on a screen, the spectators eyes and brain waves activate and a direct physical connection emerges with the original recorded results. There is no veil of zeros and ones in between. It's truth 24 times in a second.

At the very beginning of cinema, the absence of industrial labs meant that the filmmaker had to work on all stages of film production, including chemical development and printing. The Lumiere Brothers' camera, which as we know was also a projector, was used as a printer as well, and the operators of the company at the time knew how to film, develop the negative, and expose, develop and then project a positive print.

I am convinced that to invent a technique like that, someone must have a passion for it. The independent analog filmmakers nowadays kept this secrets and the innovative approach in order to keep on creating this kind of magic.

The next aspect of cool that I can connect with this topic is the form of resistance. As Dick Pountain and David Robins write in their book Cool Rules. The Anatomy of an Attitude cool can be seen as a form of resistance. Independent analog filmmaking does not just refuse to work within the commercial film industry, it also refuses to use new technologies, like the digital one. Peter Tscherkassky, an Austrian experimental filmmaker, explains in an interview why he still works with analog techniques.

These forms are not just new and innocent, but were designed to replace analog film and analog film as a medium of fine art cannot be replaced by digital technologies since the materiality of the two media are completely different and have nothing to do with one another. I decided to make work that illustrates and celebrates the qualities of analog film which cannot be replaced by non-analog media.

So this form of resistance is not just there to be against the mainstream, it is because the filmmaker really believes in what he or she is doing and continue this practice. László Nemes, director of Son of Saul and winner of the Grand Prix 2015 at the Film festival in Cannes said in an interview,

"When there's no more film, then I will stop making movies and do something else. [...] You can never compare pixels to photochemical grain that lives from one image to the next and cannot be controlled. I don't think human experience should be recorded only in zeros and ones. I think that kills the life within the image."

The same opinion is shared by successful and famous directors of big budget movies like Quentin Tarantino and Christopher Nolan. These filmmakers have the savoir of the material's originality and authenticity in common. But also the resistance against commercial production forms is important to mention. Artist-run film labs were created to bring people together, to share not just the expensive equipment and working spaces, but also to share their specific knowledge with each other. It is a form of underground movement, a community that works not necessarily against the industry, but surely not with it. It is detached from it and follows its own rules. Pip Chodorov, experimental filmmaker, co-founder of L'Abominable in Paris and distributor of analog avant-garde films explains in an interview with filmkorn. org that this alternative film scene and its work is definitely a resistance against globalization. Not what the films show, but how they are created is a form of grass roots activism, it is more ecological than economical.

This brings us to the most important element of cool that can be found in this form of filmmaking: Savoir. In order to make films the filmmaker needs a lot of know-how, he or she has to know how to use film material, how to work with a camera but he or she also needs information about chemistry and different developing processes. The independent analog filmmaker is an artist, a technician, and a chemist at once and the only way to learn this practices is by doing it, by getting the experience. But even though filmmaking requires some rules, the filmmakers don't always follow these rules. As already mentioned, they kept the innovative and ingenious approach of the early pioneers and experiment with new ways in order to create a certain style and come up with a their own thing. To come back to Peter Tscherkassky, he works mainly with found footage material and transforms it in the dark room into something different. Like in a remix, he uses already existing elements and makes something new out of it.

He works on his films one metre at a time. That's the width of his work-bench, and a reasonable way to segment his schedule. In a darkroom, he uses found footage like a stencil, masking areas of the raw film stock and then using a laser pointer or flashlight to expose his film to portions of a frame from the found footage.

Richard Tuohy and Diana Barrie from the Australian lab Nanolab apply developing chemistry with a brush on the film strip to make alternating positive and negative images. Carolee Schneemann created her film Fuses through direct animation, that means she works directly on the film material by painting, scratching or drawing on it.

There are uncountable independent filmmakers out there, that use their savoir for their projects. Ideas reach from attempts to create own film material and emulsion to cook film or let it get moldy in a wet basement. A film lab is nothing else than the necessary environment for the filmmaker to try out new things and a gathering place for like-minded artists.

[They] are drawn to the 'home-brew' DIY spirit that celebrates the autonomy of artist-run labs. Josh Lewis, who in 2012 founded the Negativeland lab in Ridgewood, Queens, describes it as 'a more involved way of being a filmmaker. You can't rely on an industry that serves Hollywood.'

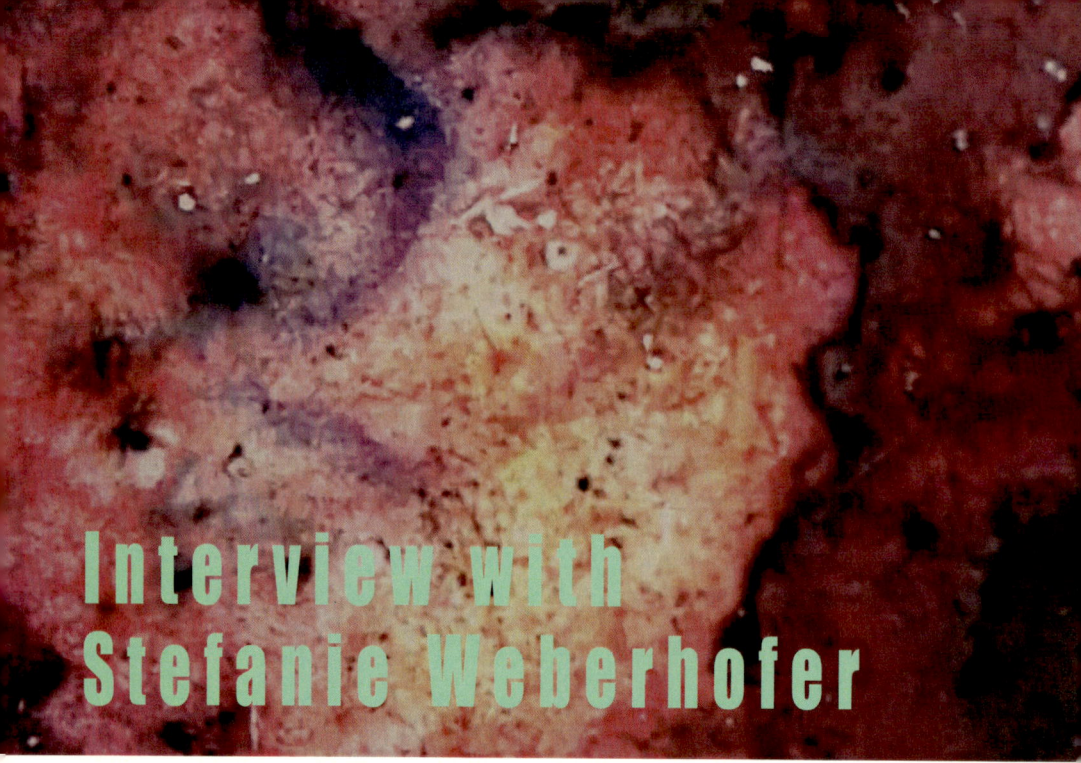

Interview with Stefanie Weberhofer

What's your background as an artist? How did you start working with film?

It all started as a game when I was a kid. I borrowed my uncle's video camera and my cousin and I started filming. I just never stopped playing that game. As soon as I realized that game could also be a real job opportunity I decided to go for it. I studied multimedia arts with a focus on video. There, I developed a very commercialized view and unfortunately also lost a bit of passion for filmmaking. After I graduated in 2012 a friend invited me to Filmkoop Wien, an artist run film lab in Vienna, Austria. It was the first time I had contact with analog film.

I was instantly fascinated, and it also turned out that film was the perfect media to start playing that game again and get my enthusiasm back. I joined filmkoop wien as a member and started exploring. I learned everything by myself - after university I didn't want anyone to tell me how to make films anymore. I wanted to find it out by myself. I spent a lot of time in the darkroom. In the first year I had no satisfying results, but with time I got better and better. Now I have a routine in many processes and I am happy to share the knowledge with others in workshops and seminars.

What inspired Dissolved (Aufgelöst)?

That project accompanied me through various steps of my personal development as an analog filmmaker.

I started exploring hand processing color film, but I did not just want to make a test film. I used the chance and played a game again. I asked a friend to give me random topic, she said "Solved" (in German: Gelöst). As my mind was already preparing for the time in the darkroom with the chemicals, the idea of filming chemical processes was close. I stumbled upon a microscope, so that film was done quickly. I also called the film *Solved* and submitted it to a few festivals. After about a year I was exploring different ways of destroying film. I thought it would be a really cool idea to use the chemicals I filmed in *Solved* to destroy the film. I cut the film in three parts and exposed them to the these chemical processes. The first part was soaked in salt water for a day, the second part was cooked in boiling water, and I put the last part in my wet basement for 6 months, which made it perfectly moldy. I digitalized the final result again and *Dissolved* (German: Aufgelöst) was made. There is actually another step to this project, which i called Abgelöst (which means replaced, but the pun does not work in English anymore). I thought with *Dissolved* I changed the fundamental substance of the film: the material. With video the fundamental substance would be the code. I opened the digital version of *Solved* in a code editor and started to write poems about chemistry, which created beautiful glitches. I present all

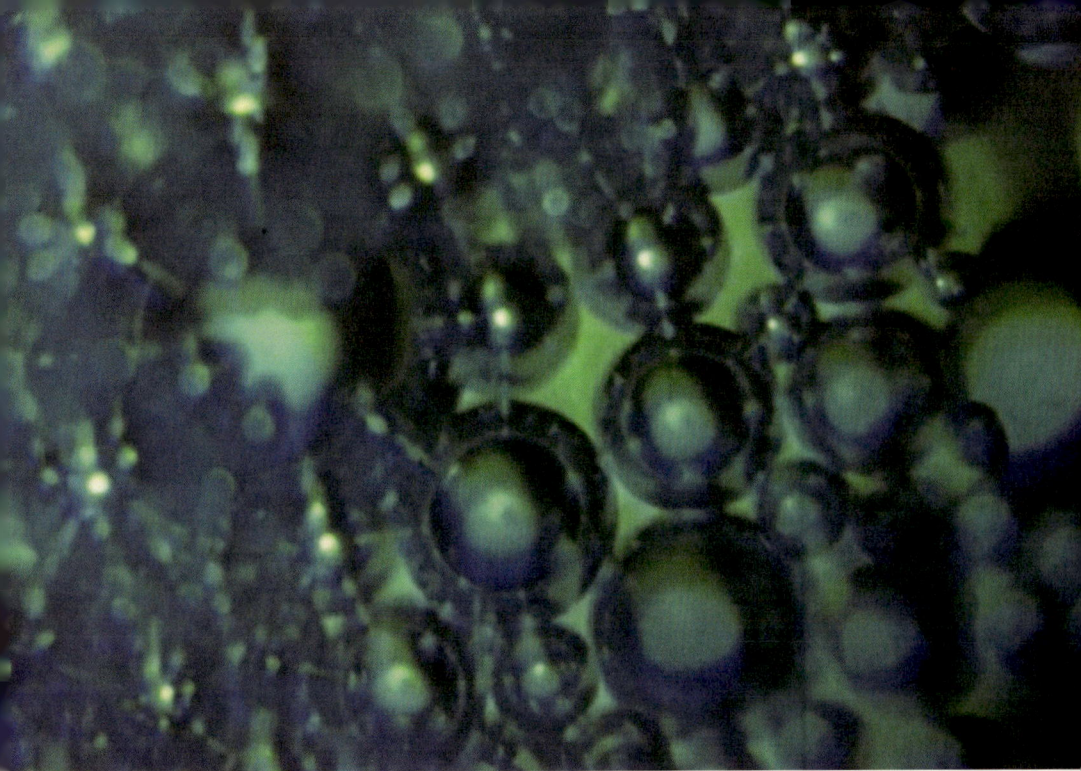

three versions as a triptychon in an installation. I love how they reflect on digital and analog decay and at the same time my personal journey at the beginning of my analog era.

What film stock did you use for Dissolved?
Expired Vision 2 50D Color Negative and it was cross-processed in Tetenal E6 (3 bath version).

Materiality seems crucial to your work. Can you tell us a bit about working with film in this way?
What's extremely important for me in my work is comprehensibility. I really want to know what happens in every step of the art I am creating. With video this is nearly impossible. At some point you end up between 1 and 0 and I really don't know, what that should mean. With film I can understand every single detail and intervene. I can break the rules or make my own. I am in charge and for me that means complete freedom. And that's crucial. That's also why all my films are hand processed. It is another step where I can be creative. I often have the feeling with video that I can only use tools that a software engineer designed, but with in the field of handmade film it is open. So, it is really more about the freedom, the materiality just comes with it. It's a great bonus.

Do you have a favorite festival or residency you've participated in?
I had a great time at La Lumiere in Montreal. I love the city and the people there.
My favorite festival is Diagonale. It's the festival of Austrian film and shows fiction, documentary, and a great selection of innovative films.

What's next for you?
I just finished my new film called Kopierwerk. It's a handmade 35mm (mostly) black-and-white structural film reflecting on the so-called obsolescence of analog media. It's made out of contact prints from found footage and photograms of analog media like newspapers, photographs, and vinyl. It's very purist, even the positive print is handmade and the sound is coming from hand-cut vinyl. I wanted to go all the way and make a statement. I have the feeling, now that this project is finished, that I will be open to new adventures. Maybe I will explore another media, like VHS or hybrid methods. I also want to make a documentary. As always there are many ideas.

FOXWOUND
SUPER SWIMSUIT

Rosalia Parra/Music Film/Super 8mm

How did you decide to shoot Fox Wound's music video on super 8?

I bought my first super 8 camera in December of 2017 and if the camera worked, I thought it would be cool to document my life and maybe make a couple short films on it. I was approached by Tyler Sidney of Foxwound to shoot their music video on Super 8, so I was super pumped to use it. The had seen the first roll I shot on my trip to Mexico City, so they thought it fit with their idea for the music video.

How did you come up with the look for the music video?

The places to shoot were suggestions of the band. Those were all prominent locations in Atlanta and places where they hang out. They wanted it to be more personal but also familiar to people local to Atlanta.

You showcase such quintessential Atlanta spots! What was your favorite location to shoot in?

I think my favorite location to shoot was probably on Jackson bridge. That spot is super touristy but looking back at that location, it explains why so many take photos there. If you get there on a good day when no one is around and right at sunset its nice to take it all in.

You mentioned you're a student. What are you studying? What do you hope to do after you graduate?

I am currently studying finance after switching multiple times (first major was French). After I graduate, I plan on continuing my pop up, and making a band. But mostly I'm excited to edit and shoot more on my super 8 camera.

What's next for you? Any other music videos coming up that we should know about?

I shot a music video for Atlanta indie pop band Pike Co. for their song *Body of the World* around this time last year that was really fun to shoot. I'm currently editing a tour video I took last year of local punk bands Drool and Harmacy but school has been making the process longer than I'd like. I'm also finishing a roll I shot last December of my mother's hometown in Mexico that I'm really excited to see, especially because it's not a commonly photographed place.

Anything else to add?

I'm very new to the whole directing, shooting and editing, but I plan on sticking to it. There is already such a big lack of women filmmakers and I think we have stories to share that are vital. Initially when I thought of myself directing films, I imagined creating fantastical movies like Pan's Labyrinth, but I think the stories I want to share for right now need to be more personal. I plan on creating films that create commentary of feeling like the "other" in the United States as well as in Mexico, just because it's something that I don't think we hear about enough. Especially not in cinema or from a women's point of view.

Printing
digital
video to
16mm film

Mega Bog "For The Old World"
Music film by Laura Conway

"

I think it's really useful to see how the same image changes going from digital onto film. I didn't know what to expect with each film stock so we tried a few. 400D was so clean it became more like a film-filter. Using Agfa our cheap rental Knight costume looked timeless. We were world building with this film and celluloid was the final feature, it added to the atmosphere to this world.

"

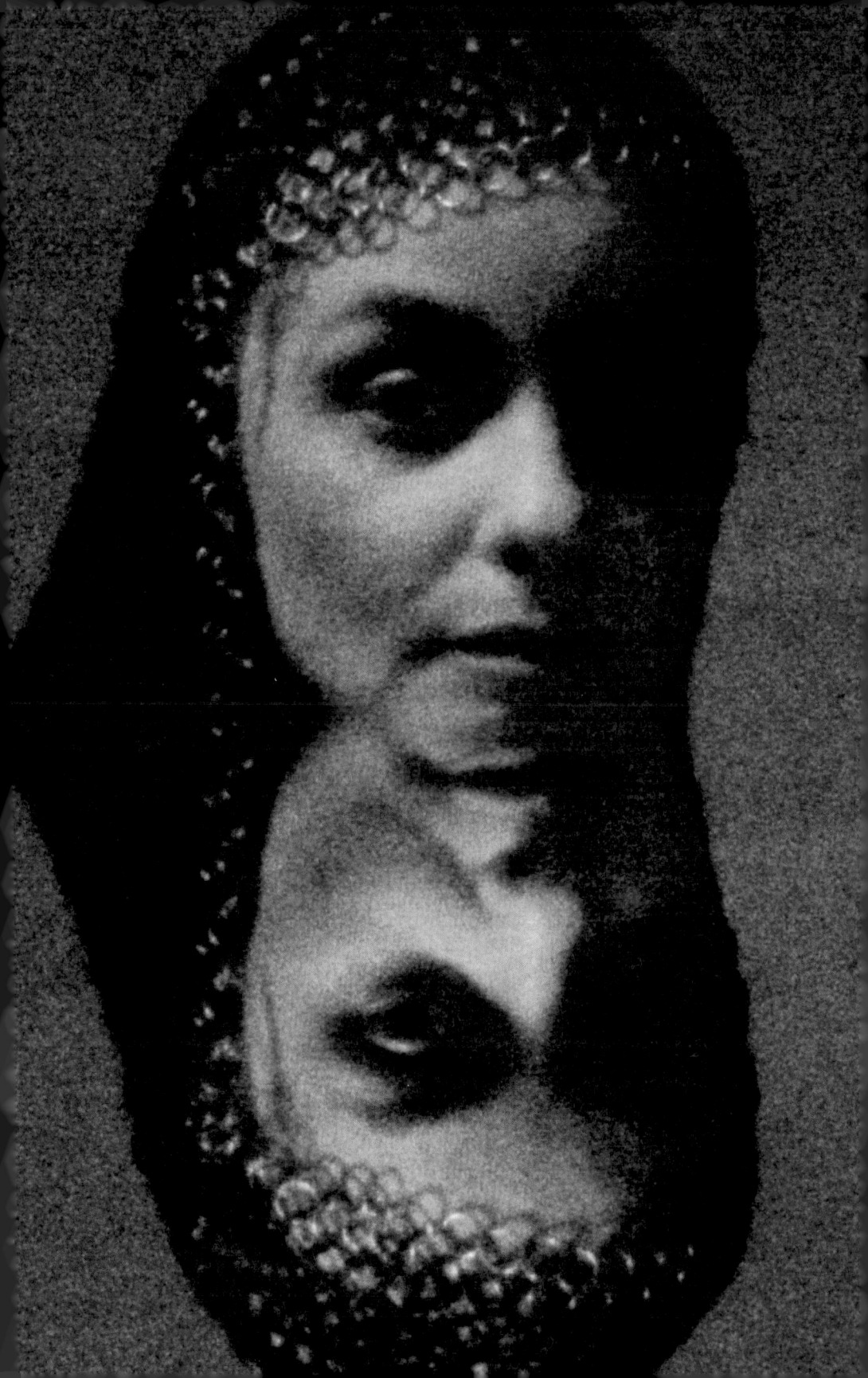

Guide to Processing
16mm Kodak B/W Reversal

with assorted wisdom on troubleshooting and technical experiments

By Nikola Dyulgyarov and Tish Stringer

Overview

Processing 16mm b/w cine film can be a daunting challenge and often, one is forced to settle for less than ideal results when faced by the numerous variables they have to keep in mind. Any deviation from the standardized development procedure will result in a poorer image. However, we are experimentalists, and those deviations are tools and free us to play with the medium. With a few precautions, one should be alleviated of the fear of developing and can focus on the image, story, composition, and plot of their film, rather than being weighed down with worries.

We believe that a rudimentary but fundamental understanding of the physical processes enables an instinctive response to problems. We intend to provide both a descriptive procedure for the dedicated few and a "cheat sheet" processing and troubleshooting guide for those who wish to make films, as well as to include some practical tips and experiments.

A crash course in photographic physics and chemistry

Black and white film is made up of a film emulsion (which contains light-sensitive silver halides AgX in gelatin) and a film base, made of plastic. You can tell them apart in the dark by putting the strip between your lips. The side that sticks to your lip is the emulsion, which has a matte luster, whereas the base side is slick and shiny.

When you correctly expose and develop ANY black-and-white emulsion, you will get a NEGATIVE image, made of silver.

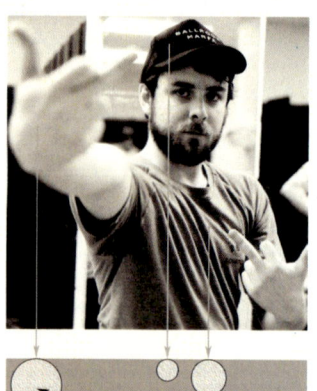

Depending on the amount of light that hits the film, a proportional amount of silver halide is converted to black silver metal.

Exposed silver halide

Film Base   Silver Halide

Developer

The result is a negative, more exposure means darker image on the film.

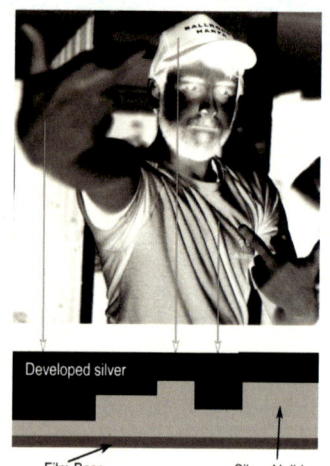

Developed silver

Film Base   Silver Halide

After the image is developed, we would normally dissolve away the remaining AgX in a fixer, because AgX are milky in color and our image will look blurry. This makes a black and white NEGATIVE.

Of course, we want a POSITIVE image, where the amount of silver is inversely proportional to the amount of light. And the solution is pretty trivial. Turns out, the amount of AgX that remains and we would normally remove by fixing is the inverse! So, imagine we could remove JUST the silver we have developed, and retain the halide. And we can, using a bleach (not the household variety, but just as dangerous).

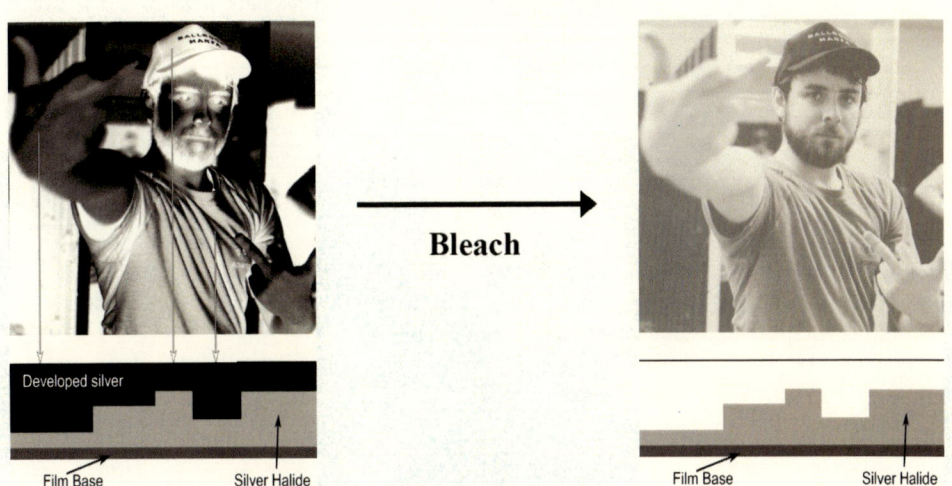

We are almost there! Notice that we don't have a perfect image. It's still made of AgX, and if you look at the film, it will look like a milky-white-yellow pale POSITIVE.

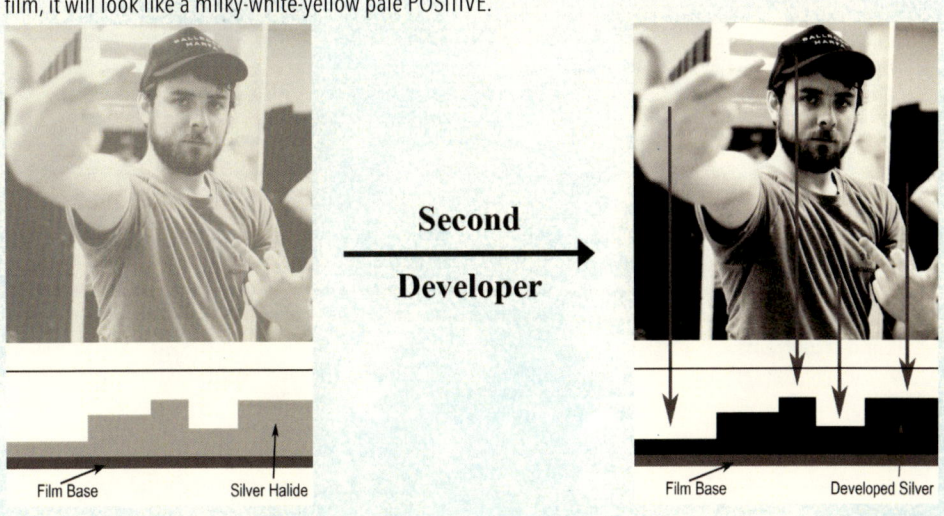

Now, we give our film so much light that all of the remaining AgX is exposed and we develop it again. And there it is, a POSITIVE in all its projection glory and detail on our 16mm strip. We then fix the film (out of habit and for archival reasons), wash it really well and dry the stock.

That is it! There are essentially four steps to processing reversal film – develop, bleach, expose to light, redevelop (second developer). In reality, we will include more steps, which are necessary so that our image looks good and does not degrade and to make sure our chemicals can be reused. All the steps are listed below in sequence with their purpose.

#	Name	Role	In the dark?
1	**Water Presoak**	Allows the gelatin to swell and let chemicals in and out. Prevents blotches.	**YES**
2	**First developer**	Develops the NEGATIVE image. MOST IMPORTANT STEP. MAKES OR BREAKS THE IMAGE	**YES**
3	**Water Rinse**	Washes away the developer chemicals	**YES**
4	**Bleach**	Etches away the negative image, leaves a positive.	**YES**
5	Water Rinse	The bleach is nasty stuff. We want to remove as much as possible.	NO
6	Clearing Bath	The bleach stains the film orange. This "clears" the stain.	NO
7	Water Rinse	You get the point…	NO
8	Re-exposure	We give the film a ton of light, to make sure all AgX is exposed.	DEF NO
9	Second Developer	Develops the final POSITIVE image.	NO
10	Acid Fixer	Makes the image stable, and the gelatin more durable	NO
11	Final Rinse	The longer the better. Any fixer that remains in the film will slowly eat away at your masterpiece and in a decade's time, it will be faded.	NO
12	Photo Flo	This is like dish soap for film. It lets the water drip away faster and not form any spots when you hang it to dry.	NO

About a dozen steps! With some exercise, the whole process can be done in a few laid-back hours to some good music. Just PAY ATTENTION to the order of chemicals and the FIRST DEVELOPER, because it determines much if not everything about your final image.

Preparation and tests: advice

0. The essentials – darkroom, equipment, supplies

In an ideal world, everyone would have access to a dedicated permanent darkroom. These have become an endangered species in the 21st century, but many creative solutions exist. If a room can be made completely dark, is spacious enough for 1-2 people to work comfortably in, and has running water (a big sink is nice), it is a good candidate. Although kitchens often fit this description, we deal with chemicals you do not want in your food, so kitchen ≠ darkroom.

Vessels and accoutrements: In processing, we need to store, measure, and transfer a lot of liquids. Plastic bottles and jugs made from HDPE or PET are airtight and don't break if you drop them. Other essentials are graduated cylinders and beakers in different sizes, funnels, stirring rods.

Tools: a good digital scale (capacity 500-1000g, resolution 0.1/0.01 g). Kitchen scales are a last resort and source of errors and doubt, avoid. A timer/darkroom clock with luminous dial is useful, but not critical (nowadays, we have excellent timers in our phones). A hotplate/magnetic stirrer removes the burden of manual mixing.

Materials: photographic chemistry can be obtained online or locally from numerous providers. Dedicated chemical reagent suppliers exist, but they often sell in bulk, have higher prices, and do not service individuals. For preparing solutions, distilled, deionized, or reverse-osmosis water is recommended and preferred.

1. Once you have shot your reel of film, there are two ways to process it:

The BUCKET process: unspool 100ft of film in a large bucket (IN THE DARK), pour the chemical and slosh around with your (gloved) hands, pour the chemical out, pour in the next chemical, etc.
Pros: less threatening, simple, a bucket with a well-fitting lid is obtainable from paint or restaurant supply stores
Cons: your film WILL get scratched, more or less, even development is not guaranteed, uses WAY too much chemicals, messy. You have to work in ABSOLUTE DARKNESS for the first 4 steps.

The LOMO tank process: load 100ft of film in two plastic reels of 50ft (IN THE DARK), put them in the Russian tank, put on the lid (LIGHTS ON), add/drain the chemicals in order, etc.
Pros: clean & even development, uses less chemicals, no mess.
Cons: OH MY HOW DO I USE THIS SOVIET CONTRAPTION??!? The loading process is kind of complicated…Youtube and dry runs with exposed film in the light are your friends, because it's worth it!

2. Tests are everything!
How do you know your chemicals work? A blank roll of film

where your senior thesis footage should be? NO!!! There are several simple tests to make sure the chemicals you have are functional (at ROOM TEMPEATURE: 69-74 F, check with a thermometer).

The CLIP test: grab a piece of scrap UNEXPOSED film (from the end of a spool or while loading the camera). Get 5-8 inches, it will be plenty. Soak the film in some water and simply dip it in the FIRST developer for a minute and agitate it. Does it turn black all the way? Your developer is good to go. If it just turns gray or stays the same, DO NOT USE the developer, as it is exhausted or expired! Don't throw the black strip away, though. Wash it with water and dip it in the bleach; it should slowly dissolve all the black and leave you a clear film strip, stained orange. If it does, then you're golden; if not, something is wrong! These two tests take less time to carry out than to read the instructions for doing them, so DO THEM! It doesn't hurt to check the SECOND developer too, but you will be inspecting the film in the light, you'd know on the spot if it doesn't work well.

The SNIP test: shoot 5-10 feet of correctly exposed film (whatever you deem correct, for Kodak 7266 it is 200ASA, but you may want to be a deviant, see below). Shoot a scene with a good range of light – shadows, gray tones, bright areas (an exterior with sky, land, and buildings works well). Cut away this strip in total darkness and store it in a light-tight bag or container. When you want to test your chemicals, use a film tank or beaker for the solutions and 5-10 inches of your correctly exposed film. Carry out the complete processing steps with the recommended times. This lets you troubleshoot any problems and adjust for them yourself (maybe you need less time in the first developer, or more in the second, etc…follow the troubleshooting guide for adjustments). Clearly, this is more involved and time consuming, but can still be done in 30-40 minutes and can save you days of filming and expensive film stock. It is also a way to familiarize yourself with the entire process before you develop your first reel. Your call.

3. Prepare your chemicals.

Check the TEMPERATURE! Chemical processes run slower in the cold and faster when it's hot! The only step that is temperature sensitive is, of course, the first developer (FD). Check the FD temperature and the chart on the instruction sheet for determining how long to develop.

Put your solutions in order! Instead of worrying which step comes next, order the bottles and jugs in sequence in the sink. Left-to-right works for me, but come up with your own system, as long as it does not involve color-coding or mnemonics.

Run a CLIP test. Just do it.

4. During processing.

Agitation is important. Slosh your film around with your (gloved) hands if using buckets or turn the LOMO reel clockwise (slow is ok) continually. The LOMO tank also lets you lift and lower the reel a tiny bit. That helps dislodge air bubbles that could ruin the perfect look you're going for. Tapping the bucket or tank gently on the sink/table also helps.

Filling and draining the LOMO tank can be done from the top lid or the draining hose. I prefer using the hose with a funnel stuck inside it. With the tank empty, lift the hose above the tank with one hand and pour the chemical though the funnel with the other. Then, pinch the end of the hose so it doesn't leak and secure it in the little loop. To drain, lift the tank (spill danger!), pinch the hose, take it out of the hoop and into the mouth of the CORRECT container, unpinch and let gravity take its course. Tilt the tank so that you get as much of the liquid out as possible.

Always start the timer AFTER the entire bucket/tank is full and all the film is submerged. Always drain AFTER the timer ends. The times listed take this into account.

Drain your chemicals completely to avoid contamination. Again, the FD is most sensitive to contaminants, so make sure you either have it in the clean bucket/tank or its storage container.

Pay attention to the image on your film. After step 4, you can turn the lights on (for bucket development) or remove the lid (LOMO tank). All following steps can be done by inspection (you can still timer them but decide to end earlier). Visual indicators are mentioned in the instruction sheet and the troubleshooting guide.

How to perform the water rinses

Bucket: fill the bucket to completely cover the film, agitate and set the timer. After 1 minute, drain the water, fill again, repeat until timer ends. Alternatively, place a water hose reaching the bottom of the bucket and allow the water to overflow, agitate with your (gloved) hands.

LOMO: fill the LOMO tank with water using the LOMO tank drain hose, so that the water exits from the top or through the lid if it still is closed). A gentle, tame flow is sufficient. Turn the reel clockwise every minute for the duration of the timer.

How to perform the re-exposure step:

Use a 100W tungsten (or equivalent CFL/LED) bulb. The while light in the darkroom may be sufficient, depending on its power and distance. A desk lamp with a 15W LED bulb is convenient and portable.

Alternatively use a 500W floodlight.

Bucket: you can either drain the last water rinse or leave the film submerged. I prefer the second option. Bring the bucket up to the light (or vise versa) for 1 minute at a distance of 1ft. Then move the film around and bring it up for 1 minute. Repeat for a total of 5 min. If using a floodlight (careful: water and electricity) place the bucket on the floor and shine the floodlamp from a distance of at least 2ft for 30 seconds. Agitate and repeat three more times for a total of 2:00 min.

LOMO: take the spool out of the tank, drain the water and bring it to the lamp. Rotate the spool at a distance of 1ft for 6 min. Try to get 3 min on both sides of the reel. Alternatively, expose with a floodlamp from a distance of at least 2ft for 30 sec on each side for a total of 2 min. Rotate the reel for even exposure!

Bucket: fill the bucket to completely cover the film, agitate and set the timer. After 1 minute, drain the water, fill again, repeat until timer ends. Alternatively, place a water hose reaching the bottom of the bucket and allow the water to overflow, agitate with your (gloved) hands.

LOMO: fill the LOMO tank with water using the LOMO tank drain hose, so that the water exits from the top or through the lid if it still is closed). A gentle, tame flow is sufficient. Turn the reel clockwise every minute for the duration of the timer.

5.After processing

Transfer the film to a drying rack, making sure it does not twist or knot. This can be tricky. Practice. For the LOMO tank, the easiest thing to do is disassemble the LOMO reel and take out the film as one (2x50ft) wet roll, place it in a clean bucket with water and a bit of Photo Flo and spool it from there! If a rack is not available, the wet film can be spooled onto a 16mm reel and transferred to the drying location.

Drying the film: just give your film time. You can touch the emulsion side to determine when its dry and the gelatin is smooth and not sticky. Several hours works well. Don't go check on your film every 10 minutes. The less movement in the room, the less dust on your film. If you do want dust on your film, then get creative.

....

Kodak 7266 Reversal Film Processing Guide

(Exposed at 200ASA, fresh chemistry, 70F)

Step #	Chemical	Time (min)	Notes
		LIGHTS OUT	
	(unspool in bucket/ load film in LOMO, put lid on)		
	LIGHTS ON (LOMO ONLY)		
1	Presoak (WATER @ 70F)	2:00	
2	First Developer (D67 @ 70F)	7:00	See chart below for temperatures.
3	Water Rinse	5:00	
4	Bleach (R-9)	3:00	Turn lights on (remove LOMO lid) after pouring bleach. Bleaching is complete when the film looks pale orange and no black remains.
5	Water Rinse	5:00	Wash until no more yellow washes out.
6	Clearing Bath (CB-1)	3:00	
7	Water Rinse	1:00	
8	Re-Exposure	1:00 to 4:00	Bucket+Lamp = 5:00 min Bucket+Floodlamp = 2:00 min LOMO+Lamp = 6:00 min LOMO+FloodLamp = 2:00 min
9	Second Developer (D-19)	4:00	Observe darkening visually.
10	Water Rinse	2:00	
11	Fixer (Kodak Rapid Hardening Fix)	5:00	
12	Final Rinse	10-15:00	Running Water > 70F
13	Photo Flo	1:00	Bucket: 10 ml PhotoFlo LOMO: 5.0 ml PhotoFlo
	SPOOL AND DRY FILM		

Temperature conversion for fresh D-67 First Developer

Temperature	64°	66°	68°	70°	72°	74°	76°	80°
Time	NO	9:00	8:00	7:00	6:30	6:00	5:15	NO

TROUBLESHOOTING GUIDE

Problem	Causes	Notes
Film is blank. No image	Film was grossly overexposed	Check light meter settings.
	Film was grossly overdeveloped	Did you forget the film in the FD?
	Film was exposed to light	
	Incorrect order of processing	CLIP test on developers and bleach. Inspect film after bleach, there should be a milky-tan positive image.
Film is black. No image.	Film was grossly underexposed.	Check light meter settings.
	Film was grossly underdeveloped in first developer	CLIP test on first developer.
	Film was not exposed.	
	Incorrect order of processing.	
Image is very pale throughout film.	Film was overexposed.	Check light meter settings.
	Film was overdeveloped.	Reduce first developer time by 30%.
	Second developer weak.	CLIP test on second developer.
Image is very dark throughout film.	Film was underexposed.	Check light meter settings.
	Film was underdeveloped.	Increase first developer time by 40%.
	First developer weak.	CLIP test on first developer.
Dark, even, grainy staining of film.	Film was not washed and cleared properly after bleach.	Make sure to thoroughly rinse film and no yellow staining remains on the emulsion.
Uneven development. Blotchy images.	Film was not presoaked.	
	Poor agitation.	
	Insufficient water rinses.	
Low contrast dark image	First developer weak.	CLIP test on first developer. Increase time by 25%.
Low contrast light image	Too long in first developer.	Decrease time by 30%.
High contrast image	First developer too strong.	
	Temperature too high.	
Dark or clear spots on film of various sizes.	Air bubbles on emulsion.	Increase presoak to 5 min with continuous agitation. A drop of Photo Flo might help

Chemical Formulations

A word on safety and chemical mix-ups:
Some of the chemicals involved in reversal processing are nasty and mean molecules. The developer can cause contact dermatitis after prolonged use, the fixer is acidic, and the bleach contains heavy metal (and not the good kind). However, with the correct safety measures, there are no significant health hazards involved.

Washing hands after exposure is the single most important precaution one can take, and gloves can offer a false sense of security, because you can't tell what chemicals are on them. Nevertheless, wear gloves and always WASH YOUR (gloved) HANDS.

Make sure all containers are labeled. My approach is to include the formula I used, any additional changes that I have, as well as the date of preparation and my initials. This avoids confusion. Labeling the caps avoids cross-contamination.

Read the MSDS/SDS for all chemicals. These exist for your health!

A note on nomenclature: Do not confuse sodium SULFITE (Na_2SO_3) and sodium SULFATE (Na_2SO_4). Both are used in photographic chemistry but have very different functions! They are not interchangeable. This is very important for preparing the clearing bath, which requires SULFITE.

1. Developers

The First Developer (FD)
Probably the most sensitive and fickle solution that almost wholly determines the end result. Therefore, its capacity and preparation should be observed carefully. The standard formulation is provided below.

Kodak D-67		
Chemicals	Amounts (grams)	
Water (45C/120F)*	500 ml	2500 ml
Metol	2.0	8.0
Sodium Sulfite	90	360
Hydroquinone	8.0	32
Sodium Carbonate monohyd.	52.5	210
Potassium Bromide	5.0	20
Potassium Thiocyanate**	2.0 (1.5)	8.0 (6.0)
Water	to 1.00 L	to 4.00 L

* if room temperature water is used, dissolving the dry powders takes a very long time
**acts as a silver halide solvent. if SODIUM thiocyanate is used, the amounts in brackets should be added.

NOTE: D67 is conveniently prepared by mixing a batch of PHOTOGRAPHER'S FORMULARY "SUBSTITUTE D-19" and adding 2.0 g/L of Potassium Thiocyanate or 1.5 g/L of Sodium Thiocyanate. Thiocyanate is important in the first developer. It CANNOT be omitted without image quality suffering.

The Secon Developer (SD)

Any normal developer (without thiocyanate) works for this step. In a pinch, D76, Xtol, Rodinal, Ilford Multigrade Paper Developer, even Caffenol, will do. Conveniently, we can use the above formula without the silver halide solvent.

Kodak D-19		
Chemicals	Amounts (grams)	
Water (45C/120F)*	500 ml	2500 ml
Metol	2.0	8.0
Sodium Sulfite	90	360
Hydroquinone	8.0	32
Sodium Carbonate monohyd.	52.5	210
Potassium Bromide	5.0	20
Water	to 1.00 L	to 4.00 L

NOTE: Use PHOTOGRAPHER'S FORMULARY "SUBSTITUTE D-19" as prepared.

2. The Bleach

Kodak R-9		
Chemicals	Amounts (grams)	
Water (20C/68F)	500 ml	2500 ml
Potassium Bichromate (Anhydrous)	9.5	38.0
Sulfuric Acid (98%)	12 ml (22 g)	48 ml (88 g)
Water	to 1.00 L	to 4.00 L

NOTE: It is important to add sufficient acid of the right concentration. If lower strength acid is available, adjust the amount accordingly (e.g. 50% acid would require twice the amounts). It is normal for a precipitate to form in the bleach during use; however, if the solution is not acidic enough, this will be excessive and hinder bleaching

3. The Clearing Bath

Kodak CB-1		
Chemicals	Amounts (grams)	
Water (20C/68F)	500 ml	2500 ml
Sodium SULFITE (ANHYDROUS)	90	360
Water	to 1.00 L	to 4.00 L

4. The Fixer

It is recommended to use an acidic hardening fixer, such as Kodak Rapid Fixer with Hardener. Ilford Rapid Fixer can be substituted, but will result in a weaker emulsion that is more prone to scratches and damage.

Reversal Shenanigans and Anecdotal Evidence: Pushing Kodak 7266

Pushing film means setting the light meter at a film speed (sensitivity) higher than the manufacturer's recommendation, 200 ASA for Kodak 7266. Pushing is commonly referred to in stops. Every stop increase is equal to doubling the film speed or underexposing by the same amount (1 stop push means setting the ASA to 400 or closing one f-stop, 2 stops – 800 ASA, 3 – 1600, etc).

Although b/w reversal film has the least latitude and "freedom" of the emulsions, it still allows for gross underexposure and will produce an image. The image will have high contrast and grain, more intense the more stops you push your stock. Luckily, in terms of processing, the only adjustment we have to make is in the First Developer! A quick rule of thumb is that, for every stop we push the film, we increase FD time by 50%. And if you follow that, you will get a projectable image for up to 2 stops of pushing. However, for the best results, which in this case means the least bad image (although some may disagree), the developer formulation has to be changed, and the realm of experimentation begins. Below I'll provide a starting point for pushing film from my personal experience, many hours of tests, some chemistry background, and developing a reel of film in my backpack for one hour whilst biking the streets of Houston. Feel free to use that information at your own risk.

Film Stock	Speed (Push)	Developer	Temp	Time	Notes
Kodak 7266	200 (0)	D67 (D19 + 2.0 g/L KSCN)	72 F	6:30	baseline
Kodak 7266	400 (1)	D67 (D19 + 2.0 g/L KSCN)	70 F	11:30	
Kodak 7266	400 (1)	D67 (D19 + 1.5 g/L KSCN)	72 F	12:00	better contrast
Kodak 7266	800 (2)	D67 (D19 + 2.0 g/L KSCN)	74 F	18:00	shadows pale
Kodak 7266	800 (2)	D67 (D19 + 1.0 g/L KSCN)	72 F	22:00	good
Kodak 7266	>1600 (3)	D67 (D19 + 0.3 g/L KSCN) low agitation	70 F	60:00	dark but visible image
Kodak 7266	>1600 (3)	Ilford MG Paper Developer 1+9 0.3 g/L KSCN constant agitation	70 F	45:00	good density but lower contrast
Kodak 7266	>1600 (3)	Ilford MG Paper Developer 1+7 0.3 g/L KSCN constant agitation	72 F	40:00	best result obtained

Note: that I decrease the amount of thiocyanate (KSCN) as I increase development time. The role of KSCN is to improve image resolution, contrast, speed, by dissolving some of the undeveloped halide during development. However, this means reduced shadow density and an overall pale and low contrast image. My recommendation is to decrease thiocyanate linearly with increasing development time. So, if you increase the development time twice from recommended, decrease KSCN by half, and so on.

Addendum: other notes for the intrepid

• Avoid cross-contamination! This is a common cause of problems. Introducing even small amounts of fixer or bleach into a developer can deteriorate its properties and ruin it. Have dedicated labeled containers for storing, measuring, and transferring the developer, bleach, and fix! It is good practice to wash every vessel and implement immediately after use.

• A safer bleach: Kodak R-9 is based on a hexavalent chromium salt, which is an environmental and health hazard. Kodak now recommends and sells a bleach based on permanganate. However, our attempts at formulating and using a permanganate bleach have not been able to match the results of bichromate and we cannot recommend a formula.

• Chemical Life, Capacity:
Kodak D67 (D19) has a shelf life of 6 months when unused and stored in an airtight container. Developer in use lasts about 1 month. An estimate for its useful capacity is 1000 sq. in. of film per L (1 ft 16mm film = 7 sq. in). Fixers have a shelf-life of 6 months. It is difficult to estimate capacity, but a simple test can be used – an unprocessed strip of film is dipped in the fresh fixer and the clearing time (the time for the film to become completely clear) is recorded. Before subsequent uses, the same test is run, and the clearing time will slowly increase, which is normal. When the time becomes double the beginning, the fixer is exhausted. The bleach has an indefinite shelf life when unused. With use, it will become slower, acquire sediments and turns from yellow-orange to brown-green. Once the bleaching time exceeds 5:00-6:00 min, the bleach is exhausted.

The clearing bath should be replaced when replacing the first developer.

• Depending on the amount of film a lab processes, it might be cost-effective to replenish the working solutions instead of preparing new batches by taking out a volume of the used solution and replacing it with fresh stock. Replenishment of the developers, bleach and fixer is possible. For every 7 rolls of 30ft. film processed, replenish:
o Kodak D67 – 500 ml
o Kodak D19 (second developer) – 200 ml
o Kodak R9 – 300 ml
o Kodak Rapid Fixer – 300 ml

• Thiocyanate is a very important ingredient in the first developer! It is obtainable through most chemical and photography supply stores and a little goes a long way. Although it can be omitted or replaced with sodium thiosulfate (hypo), this is highly advised against!

• There is ample room for experimentation once the user is comfortable with the process. There are thousands of formulas and processes available in the literature and online, but it is always best to begin with a verified, known procedure before exploring these possibilities.

Charlie Mirador

35mm Photography

" The majority of what I document or like to photograph is pretty much life unfolding before my eyes. There are many occasions where I go outta my way to get involved in situations or engage with subjects just to get (that?) shot. For the most part and what I prefer, is to just let it be me, a camera, no particular destination, and my furious guide that is intuition and curiousity. "

PLAY

i spent $200* to digitize a box of VHS tapes
I had found years earlier.
abandoned in the basement of my fathers evicted home
I held onto the tapes for 8 years

my mother and I had left in a hurry,
the tapes were casualties of that particular war

i received the returned tapes marked with small stickers that read,
this tape arrived damaged
for the most part, they played just fine

i like the sound of static and white noise
that accompanies memories
which are not my own

*they were having a sale for the new year

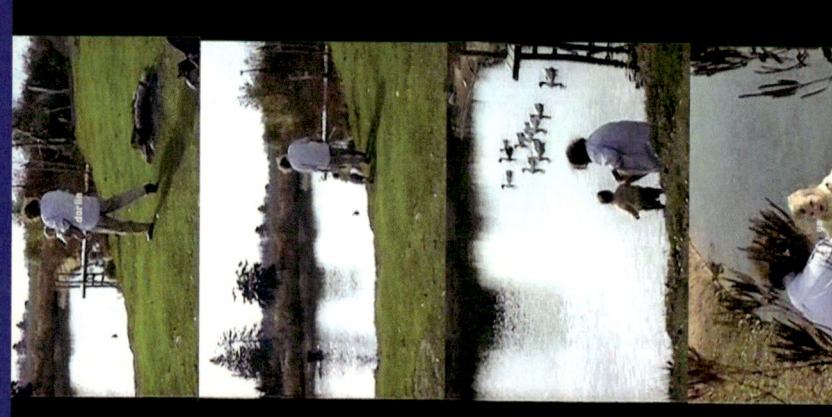

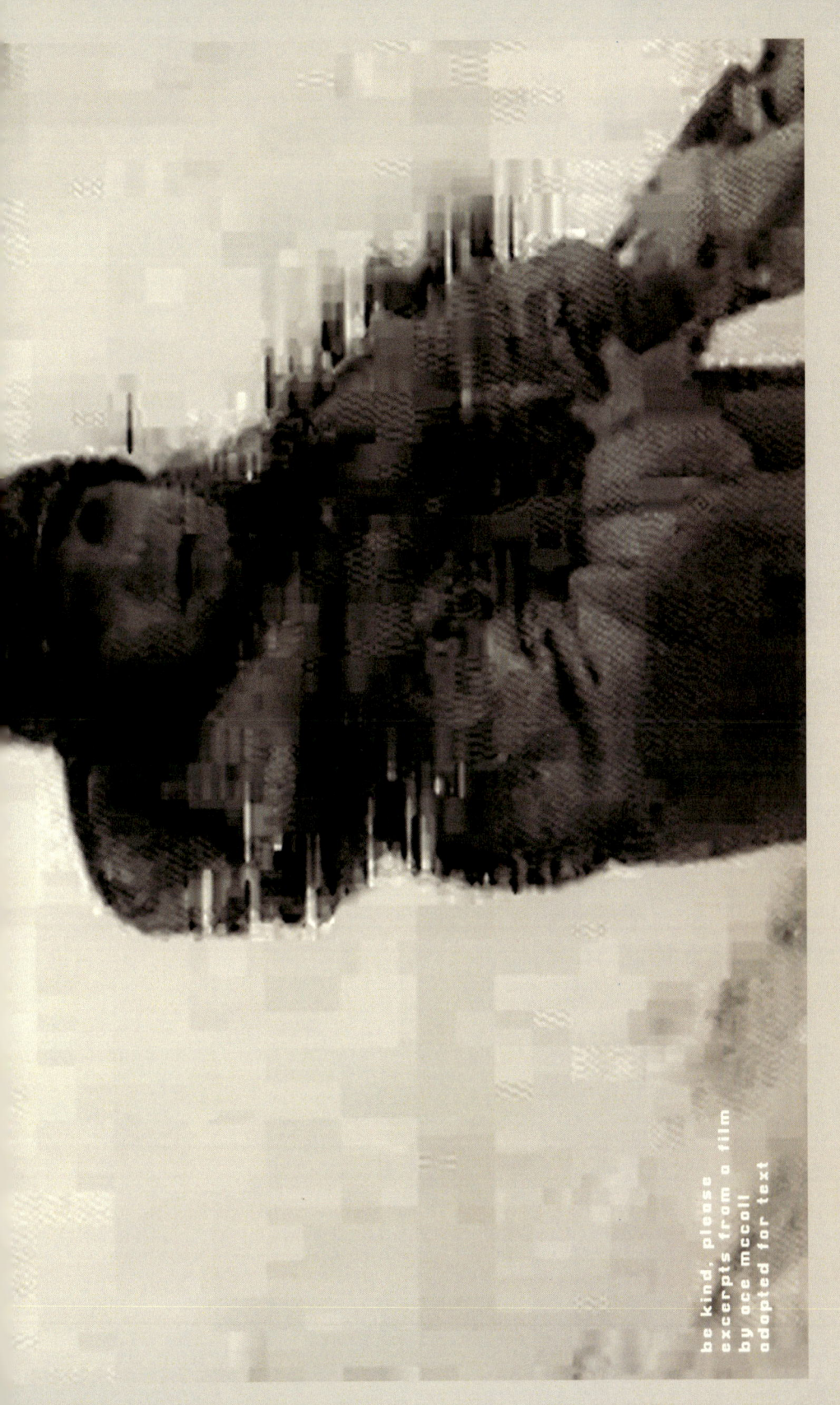

be kind, please
excerpts from a film
by ace mccoll
adapted for text

What is a Moment

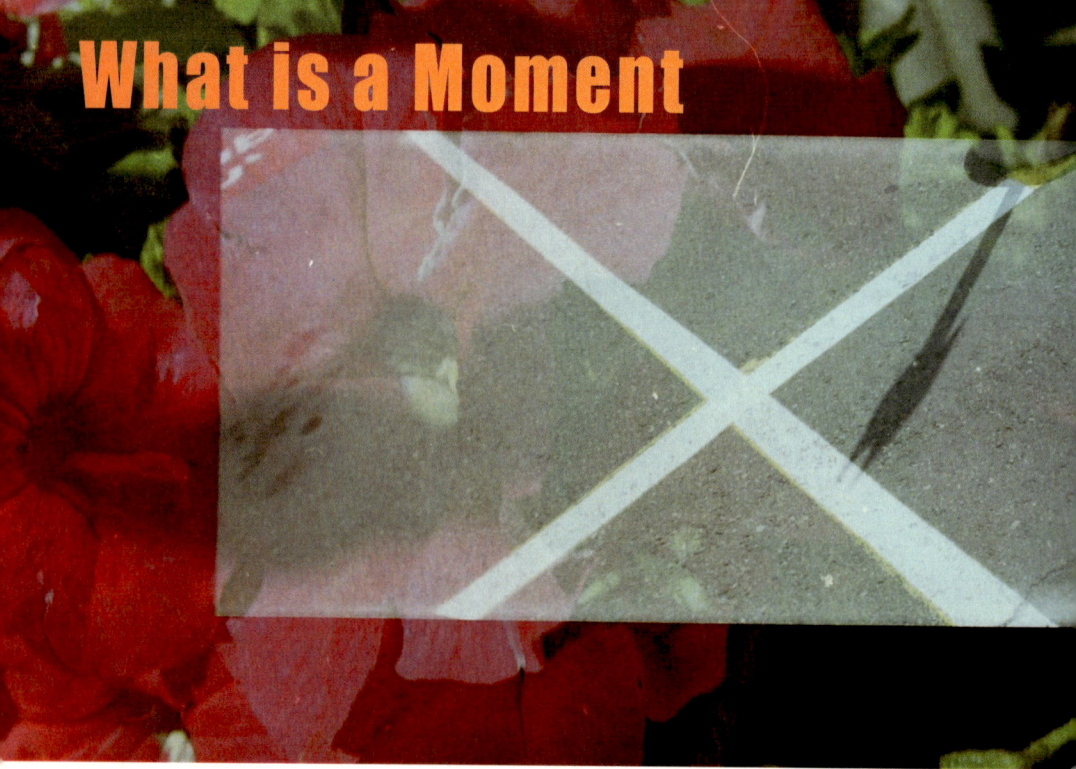

It's been a stressful fall and I'm finally getting around to developing some film. I'm guesstimating my mixing and my brother, who's hovering over my shoulder, is visibly anxious.

"The way you're doing it, you're not going to know what you get." He says.

I nod.

"That's sort of the point."

I grab my changing bag, developing tank and the two rolls I want to develop. I take a moment to explain to my brother how to open the rolls and spool them in. I put everything in the bag and zip it up.

"Do you have an old roll I can practice with?" He says as he slides his hands through the bag's arm holes, "I don't want to ruin your film."

I shrug then motion for him to start. He starts moving his hands around inside the bag. My cat, excited by the movement pounces on him.

"Oh! I think I touched the frames." He says.

"Don't worry," I say as I take my cat to another room. "It's all part of the process."

After several minutes of struggling, my brother gets the hang of it and I hear the click clacking of the spool.

"Now what?" He asks when he's finished.

I take him to the sink and give him a pair of gloves. I show him how to pour the developer into the tank.

"You have to shake it tons so the developer does its job." I say.

"How?" He asks.

"It's up to you how you want to agitate. If you shake it gently you'll get different results than if you do it aggressively because you'll create air bubbles."

He chooses a measured approach. We follow the next steps: stop bath, fixer, rinse, and squeegee.

"You should really be using distilled water for this," he says, "You're going to get streaks."

"I want streaks," I answer.

We hang the film up to dry, just out of reach of my cat's claws.

***

Mid-winter. I've been working long days and I feel like I haven't seen the sun in months. Despite the cold, I grab my camera bag and head outside. The aim of this walk is to capture my current mood. Film is expensive and I'm down to my last roll. These pictures have to count.

A few minutes in I spot the perfect setting. It's a stretch of icy sidewalk running parallel to a relatively busy street.

I take out my Canon Rebel EOS XS and set it to shutter priority. I'm shooting Kodak Gold 200 so with the dim lighting I can take a 10" exposure with an F16 aperture. I frame my shot and get my focus.

I set the timer and walk into the frame. After the shutter opens I stay in place for a few seconds. I experience the icy wind on my cheeks, the snow

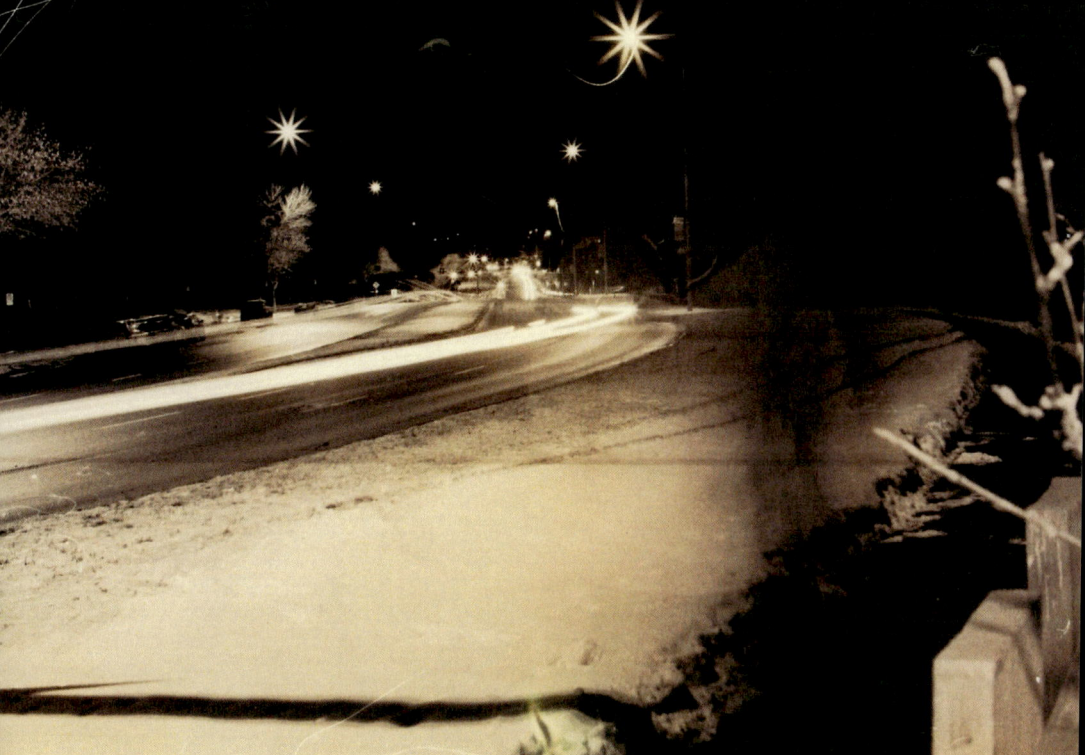

By Andrés Porras

melting in my shoes, and the cars zooming by me on the road. I count four one thousands and walk slowly out of frame. I wait until I hear the camera's motor whir and know the exposure has finished.

The resulting images show long light trails in the background with a ghostly, almost imperceptible image of me in the foreground. Streaks, cat

These happy accidents add up, creating a portmanteau of connections on the frame.

hairs, and scratches accumulated during the developing process are visible as well. These happy accidents add up, creating a portmanteau of connections on the frame.

***

So, do you think you'll want to do this yourself?" I ask my brother after all the film has been hung up.

He shakes his head.

"It's cool and all," he says, "but I think I'll stick to digital. It's just better"

I see what he's doing, he's goading me into a debate. I know I shouldn't react, that I should accept both medium's merits but I just can't.

"Film is so much richer!" I say, "You have limited shots so you have to nail every exposure!"

He laughs.

"See that's why I shoot digital," he says, "I want the flexibility. I want to know my images won't be blurry or shaky. Digital is just the best way to capture a moment."

***

It's summer now and the Calgary Stampede has rolled into town. It's a big deal in my city and the fairgrounds draw huge crowds every year.

My favorite attraction is the Motocross riders. It's exciting, adrenaline pumping fun and I want to capture it on celluloid. I have a mechanical Nikon camera with a roll of Fujicolor 400. The camera has no autofocus and I'm using the Sunny 16 rule for my exposures.

I watch the riders rehearse their jumps a couple of times, keeping one eye on my viewfinder and my second one open so I can follow the action. I want a fast shutter speed to avoid blurring which means I'll have to be precise with my focus. I pick the spot I'll be pointing at and wait. With one eye on the viewfinder I listen to the announcer and the roar of bikes. As they zoom over the ramp I wait for the right moment and click my shutter.

I get the pictures back and although I nailed the focus, they feel like they're lacking something. The riders hover in place, their feats captured for posterity, there is no sense of speed.

I return to the grounds with a roll of Rollei's Redbird Creative in my camera and a variable ND filter on my lens. I follow the same process as before except this time, I crank my ND up to the highest possible level and increase my shutter speed to 1" or 2".

The longer exposure means I have to track the riders as they fly through the air. It's trial and mostly error and of the five pictures I take, only two have defined shapes.

I put both image styles side by side. The Redbird's background speaks to the heart pounding adrenaline, the streaks capture movement. The color image speaks to the technique and precision of the riders.

Their juxtaposition allows a deeper understanding of the moment.

***

"The brain doesn't hear sound or see light." Anil Seth says in the background. "What we perceive

A picture tells a story of the moment, but it should also tell the story of itself. The minute you commit a picture to digital you've frozen it in time.

is its best guess of what's out there in the world." It's a Ted Talk I have on titled "Your Brain Hallucinates Your Conscious Reality." I'm playing it to prove a point.

I turn to my brother.

"See! That's why I shoot film," I say, "It's closer to how our brains actually work. It's not exact. It's an approximation."

"Yeah..." he says, unconvinced. "But it doesn't capture reality. You're not really grabbing the moment."

"So, then what is reality?" I ask, "Or for that matter what is a moment?"

He thinks a second.

"It's an instance in time," he says, "Although I suppose that's up for debate too."

***

It's spring and the world is in bloom. I'm a comical sight, a grown man in rollerblades, taking pictures. I know people are side-eying me but I ignore them. I have a limited amount of time before the lab closes and I want to get to as many places as I can.

The roll in my Canon used to be inside a "panoramic" film camera. I use quotations because it essentially captures a 16:9 image in a 4:3 frame, leaving black bars above and below. I shot a roll, rewound the film and transferred it to my other camera using my changing bag.

I zip from location to location. I don't quite remember what was on the original roll so I'm just looking for textures that can sit as a background to the first images.

These double exposures reveal themselves as you examine them. Because the frame lines don't align between the two cameras, I make decisions on where the picture begins and ends as I scan them.

***

Our discussion has drifted from the workings of the brain into the realm of quantum physics.

"A photon doesn't really exist until it hits a sensor," he says, "What we're doing is forcing it to go from probability to reality when we press the shutter"

"Yes," I say, "but that's not really the end of the picture."

I hold my camera in my hands showing it to him as I speak.

"A picture tells a story of the moment, but it should also tell the story of itself. The minute you commit a picture to digital you've frozen it in time."

I show him the faded leather of the camera strap.

"It can't age, it can't scratch, and it can't go into an album that someone can hold in their hands. It just stands there, sterile, telling you nothing about itself. Film is real, it's tangible, and it evolves over time."

"I guess you're right," he says.

Feeling triumph at hand, I push my advantage.

"So," I say, "Are you going to switch to film?"

"No."

Then he takes the camera from my hands, brings it up to his face, and clicks the shutter.

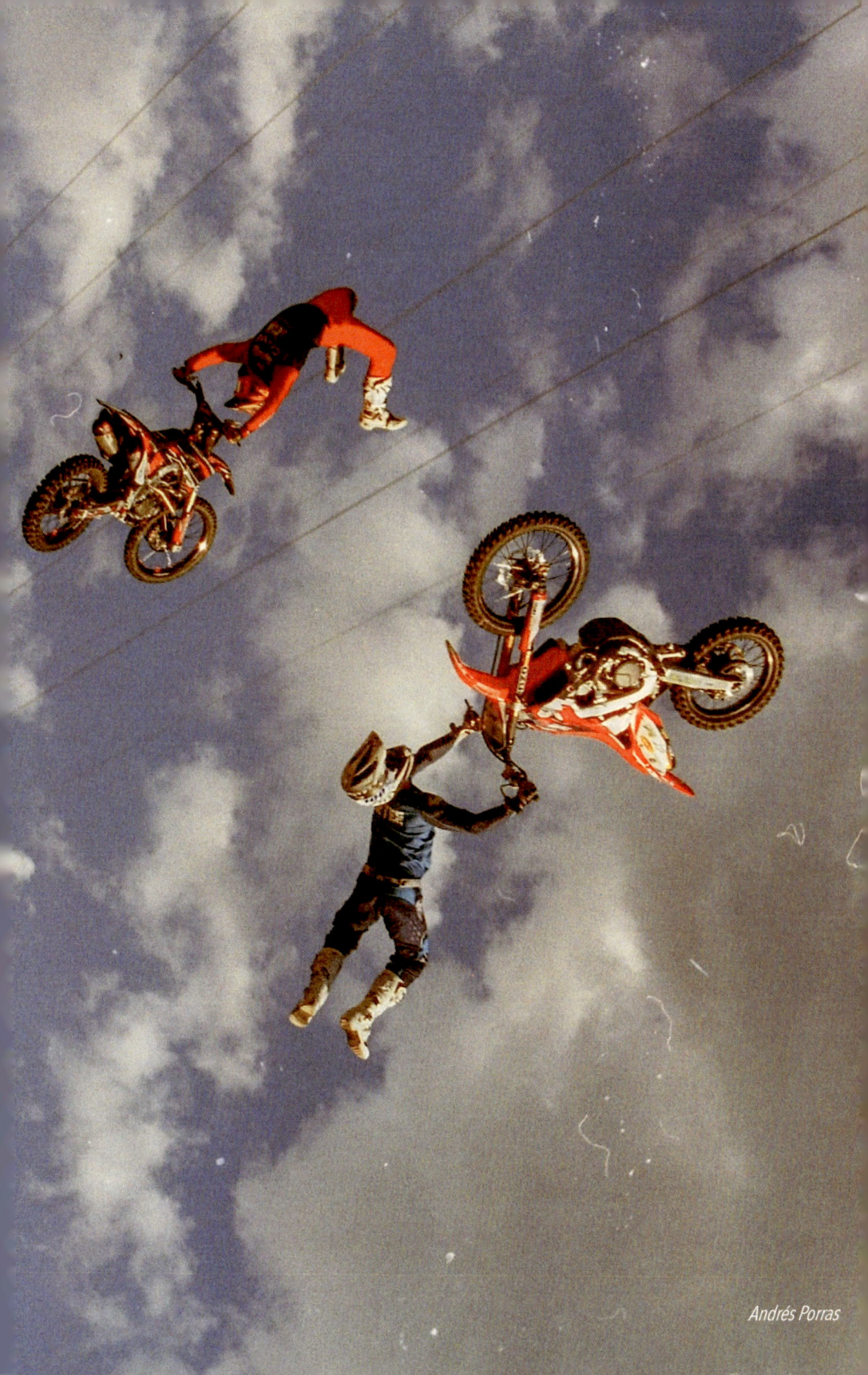

Andrés Porras

Andrés Porras

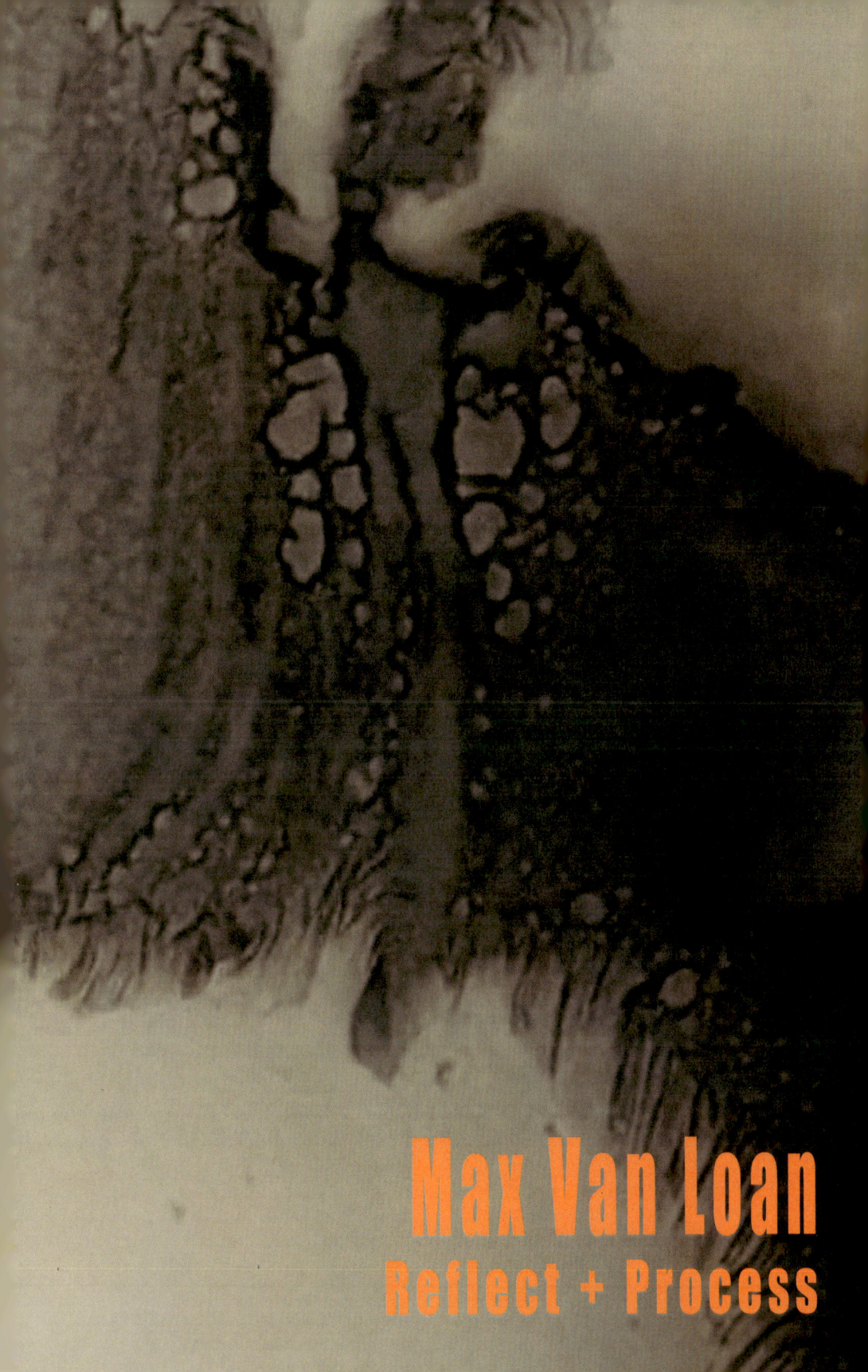

Max Van Loan

Reflect + Process

What does it mean to be a diaristic filmmaker?

At first, I shied away from the designation of my films as diary films. I felt there was a connotation of deeply personal films having less value than more conceptual, objective films. But I have since decided that embracing the identity of a diaristic filmmaker is not only accurate for the type of films I make, but also feels like a political statement about art and cinema and the value of telling personal stories. Now being a diaristic filmmaker means for me embracing the emotional closeness to myself of the content of the films I want to make. It means embracing the idea that my films are a direct representation of me and allowing the vulnerability I crave to present itself.

Who are your diaristic inspirations?

Carolee Schneemann, Gunvor Nelson, Su Friedrich, Nina Fonoroff, and Sadie Benning. I am always looking to see more!

In a *Watched Cunt Never Comes*, can you talk about the metaphor of a pot of water coming to a boil and a woman coming to orgasm?

Once, I was watching a pot of water come to a boil and I made the connection. They both start with a low warmth, that heats up and bubbles to the surface, culminating in an explosion of heat and sound, that lasts for more than just a moment, and cools down at its own pace. Of course, I have made this connection as a cis woman and I do not want to purport that I am speaking for all women, but this metaphor has been accurate for my own experience of pleasure.

Tell us about *Fool(ed) (reprise)*. Why was it important to revisit a previous film?

The previous film that I was revisiting, *Fool(ed)*, was a film that I made about my experience with sexual assault. That film was a huge endeavor for me, a therapeutic experience. I have been able to heal from the trauma for the most part, but healing is not linear, and I think we have to be okay with that. *Fool(ed) (reprise)* was born out of a moment when I was worried that that healed wound had re-opened; I felt the anger again, so I put it outside of my head and into the world.

Why Etch Bleach?

Etch bleach works by selectively destroying the parts of the image with the densest concentration of silver halides, so in a high contrast image it destroys only the darkest parts. With this image that I made during the process of creating Fool(ed), etch bleach was able to specifically destroy the optically printed and processed negative image of my body. I think it was an expression of frustration and anger that I could still get to a place of pain regarding that trauma. But the act of destroying that image helped me vent that anger and frustration and remember that it is okay for healing to be non-linear.

In Fool(ed) you interviewed someone who caused you tremendous harm. How did you do this?

Forgiveness was really important for me to move on from that harm that he caused me, so I was able to reconnect with him and have a phone conversation about what happened. He took responsibility for his actions, which I never expected. I made an audio recording of the phone call for my personal use; I think to prove to my sometimes-still-doubting self that these things happened. I ended up using the audio recording in *Fool(ed) (reprise)*.

What's your advice for filmmakers who want to tell personal stories on celluloid?

Embrace vulnerability! Vulnerability begets vulnerability, which begets connection. And connection is the whole reason we're here.

Processing Film w/a Hand Tank

- Paterson Multi-Reel 5 Tank ($42.50 B+H Photo)
  - 25ft 16mm or 50ft Super8 @ a time
- Loading the tank —

take film off spool	unwind it backwards	like this	Stuff it in the tank as haphazardly as possible

* Don't forget the little cylinder that goes in the tank → below the funnel

Emily M. Van Loan

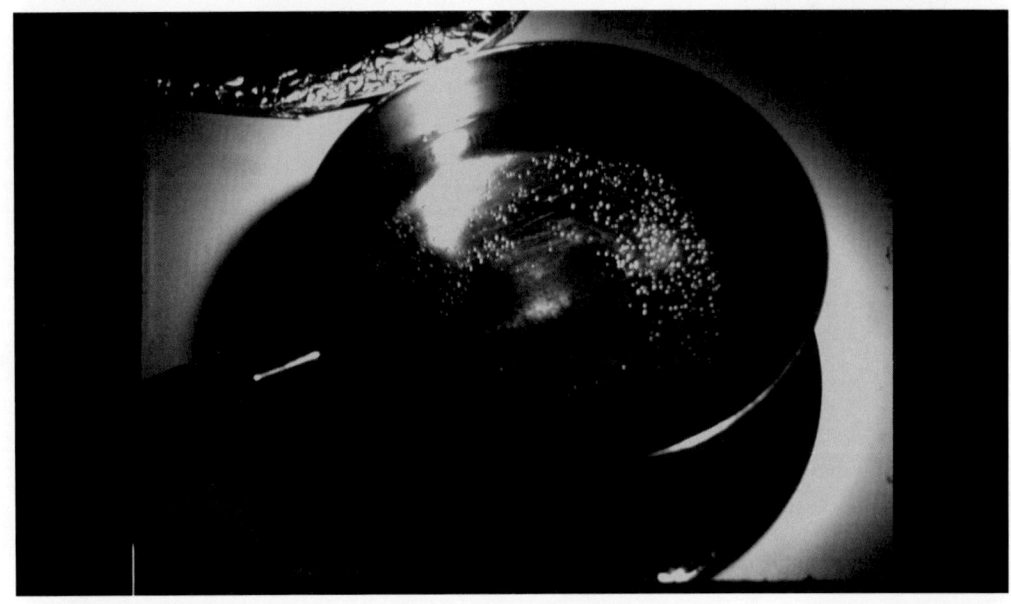

Etch-Bleach

w/ Emily M. VanLoan

Recipe

- 750 ml water
- 10-30 g copper chloride
- 80-110 ml acetic acid
- water to 1000 ml

Part A

- 4% hydrogen peroxide
- 10-20 volume

Part B

Adapted from The Experimental Photography Workbook by Christina Z. Anderson

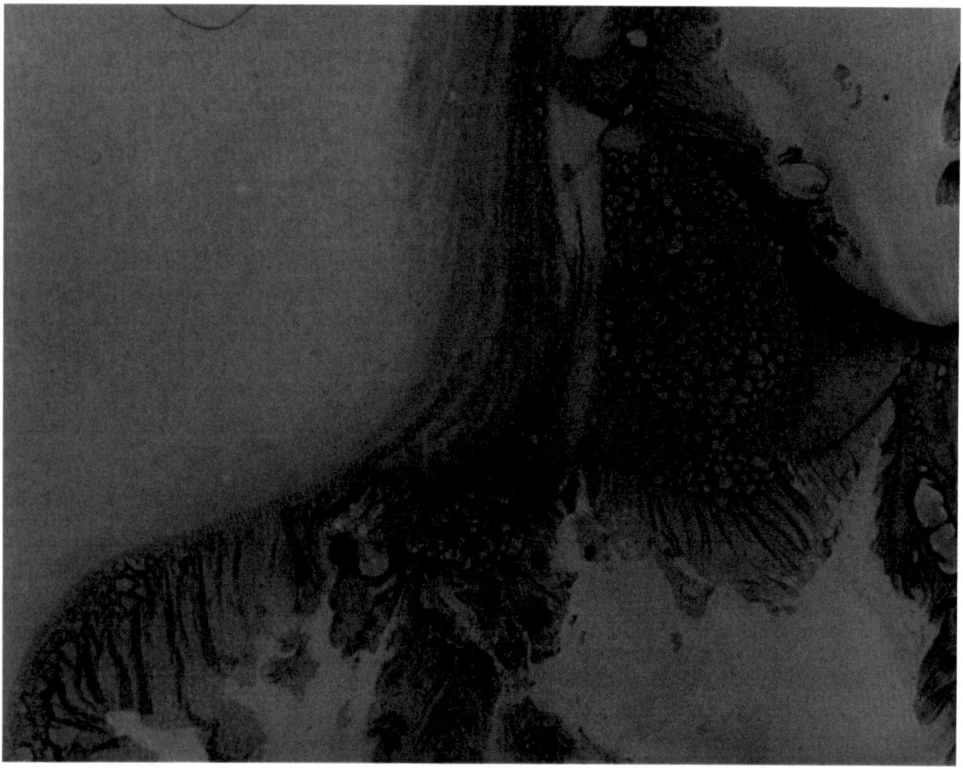

Wear Gloves!

BE CAREFUL

This Solution is Toxic

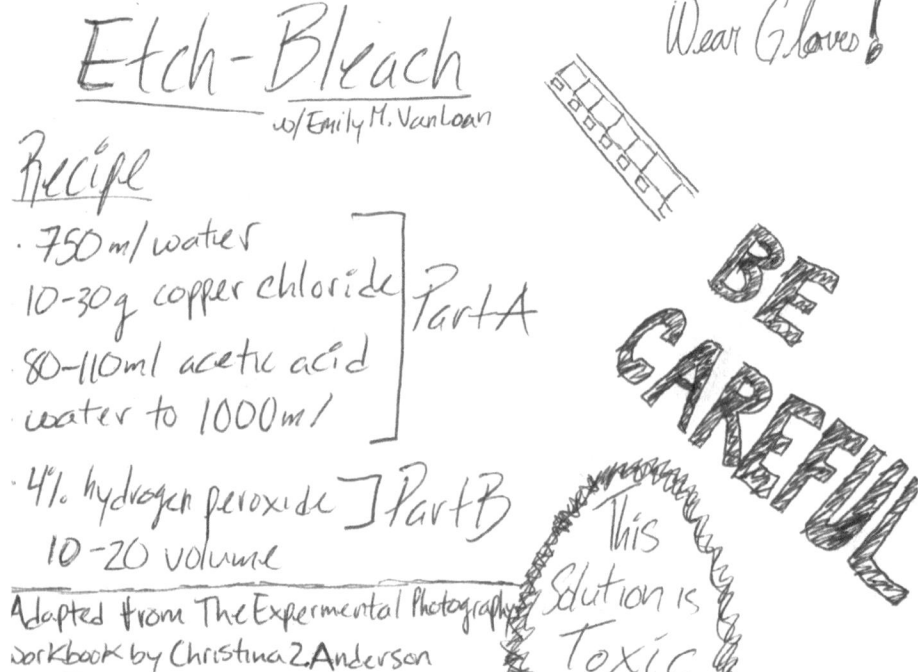

Directions

Trays set up like this ✓

this process works really well with images that have dense blacks ∵

| etch/bleach | water | Dektol 1:5 | water |

Experiment with <u>bleaching</u> time, <u>rinse</u>, re-develop (experiment with timing), <u>rinse</u> again. Hang to <u>dry</u> ⟶ scan or <u>project</u> ∵

Tip: cut film into strips to test timing/etc.

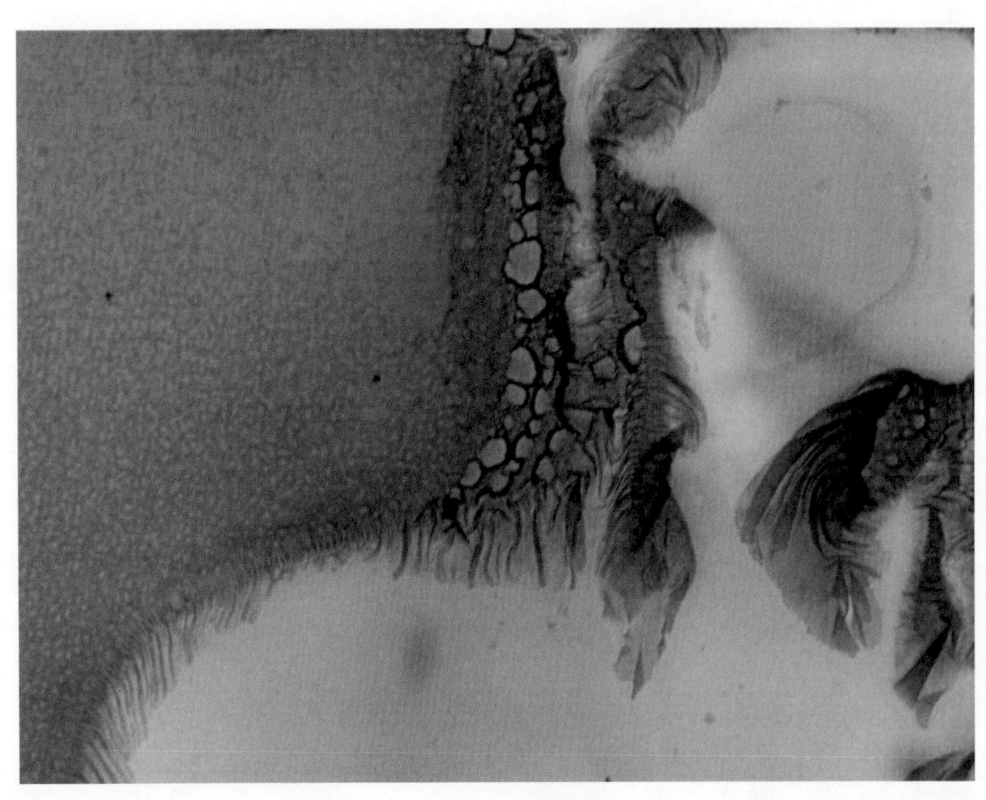

59

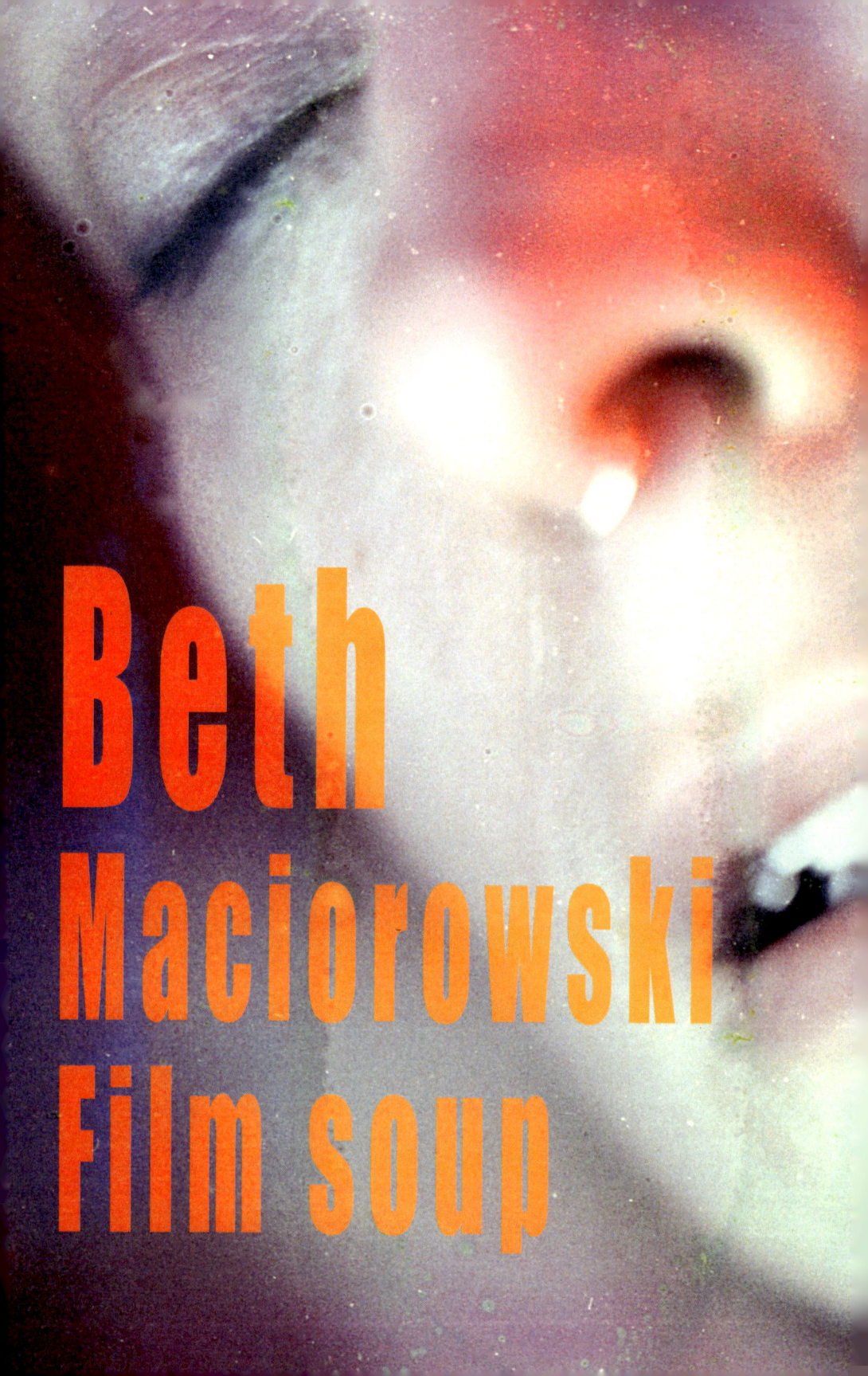

Tell us about your process - do you plan before you shoot? Do you process your own film?

I mostly shoot spontaneously and like to go outside into nature and let the surroundings inspire me. I recently shot a series that was planned out and it hasn't been my way of working in the past but I hope to try it again soon. I always process my own film at home, color and black and white. Sometimes I manipulate in the processing by using old chemicals or not using the correct times and temps. I love the magic of seeing the images on the negative strips when I take them off the reels.

Film can be very unpredicatble. Tell us about a time when you learned or evolved from a mistake.

There is an element of detachment to it and this is the biggest thing I have taken away from my experiences. I cannot get too attached to the outcome. Things could go wrong or not turn out how I'd like. This is what slows me down and keeps me experimenting. I like the saying, don't think just shoot. It is freeing.

What inspires you generally, or what inspired one or two of the pieces you've submitted?

Nature inspires me always. I love flowers and use them often In my work. I am inspired by my feelings, what I am going through, things I have dreamed about, love and loss, music and poetry. I love to travel and am inspired by visiting new places.

What are some words to live by?

The only way out is through.

What are some experiments or techniques you want to try?

Building a darkroom and experimenting with printing. Shooting both sides of the film, which I have tried a few times but want to play with more. Conceptual photography and working with models. Someday hopefully shooting large format or getting a nice medium format camera. And always, more film soup!

Super 8 / sci-fi / my Dad and me

I remember Dad blowing dust off the lid of the shoebox, being asked to turn off the lights, and feeling excited as he reached inside and unearthed the reels of cine film. To my young eyes they looked like alien objects. Or perhaps forgotten treasure. I remember watching as he threaded the tiny strip of film into the projector, before flicking the switch. There was a flash of light, a rush of hot air, and the loud whirring of the motor. After a few frames of black, images flickered on the garage wall. Like memories, they were of my Dad, looking a little younger, then my Mum, curly haired, and finally, of me, as a baby.

This is my earliest memory of my Dad's cine films. And something I always think of when making my own.

So about that. People always ask me why I make my films on super 8 cine film. Isn't it just a lot of bother? And expensive? I mean, this is the 21st century. Why not just use a 'normal' camera like everyone else? Why are you so obsessed with being analog? Why not use your iPhone?

I give different answers depending on how I feel at the time. It's the aesthetic. I love the look of cine film, the scratchy, vintage feel. The way the images blur. The colors. The nostalgia. All are correct, valid reasons. But the truth is it has something to do with that time I watched my Dad's films, on the garage wall of our old house. The sights, sounds, and smells of *real* film.

And there's another of the senses that it invokes. Touch. The way I work, I physically cut and handle the film. I wind splicing tape around my thumbs, then place it onto the celluloid, bringing the two cut edges together. I feel the smooth edge of the film in my fingers. And I feed it in and out of projectors, viewers, and rewind it back onto the reels. So, for me, the filmmaking process is tactile. Hands-on. My films aren't just digital objects; downloads and pixels. They actually exist as real physical objects.

Recently, after two years of shooting and hand editing, I finished my new film *Stella Erratica*. It's been a labor of love. My longest film to date, it took the longest to make too. And a sci-fi is all uncharted ground for me.

For the premiere we held an event at my local cinema the Silver Screen Folkestone in the south east of the UK. With its red velvet curtains, old-fashioned popcorn counter and portraits of Hollywood legends across the walls, it's like a vintage picturehouse. Nothing else says film to me more than this venue. It's my favorite cinema in the world.

The premiere was an overwhelming, unforgettable experience. The cinema was sold out. After my film had finished, as I stood there and looked across the rows of faces, I could just about make out my Dad. He was smiling at me. I could tell he was proud.

I do not want this to become slushy. Like a cheesy verse printed in a greetings card, but I argued and fell out with my Dad on my 21st birthday. Long story short: we didn't speak for almost ten years. And there were so many times I wanted to reach out to him, but I didn't. We missed so much in each other's lives. But we've reconciled now. That's in the past. But that day in the cinema, there he was, watching my super 8 film. It brought us closer. A connection. He had passed that analog baton to me, and I could tell he was genuinely proud.

Ben Barton

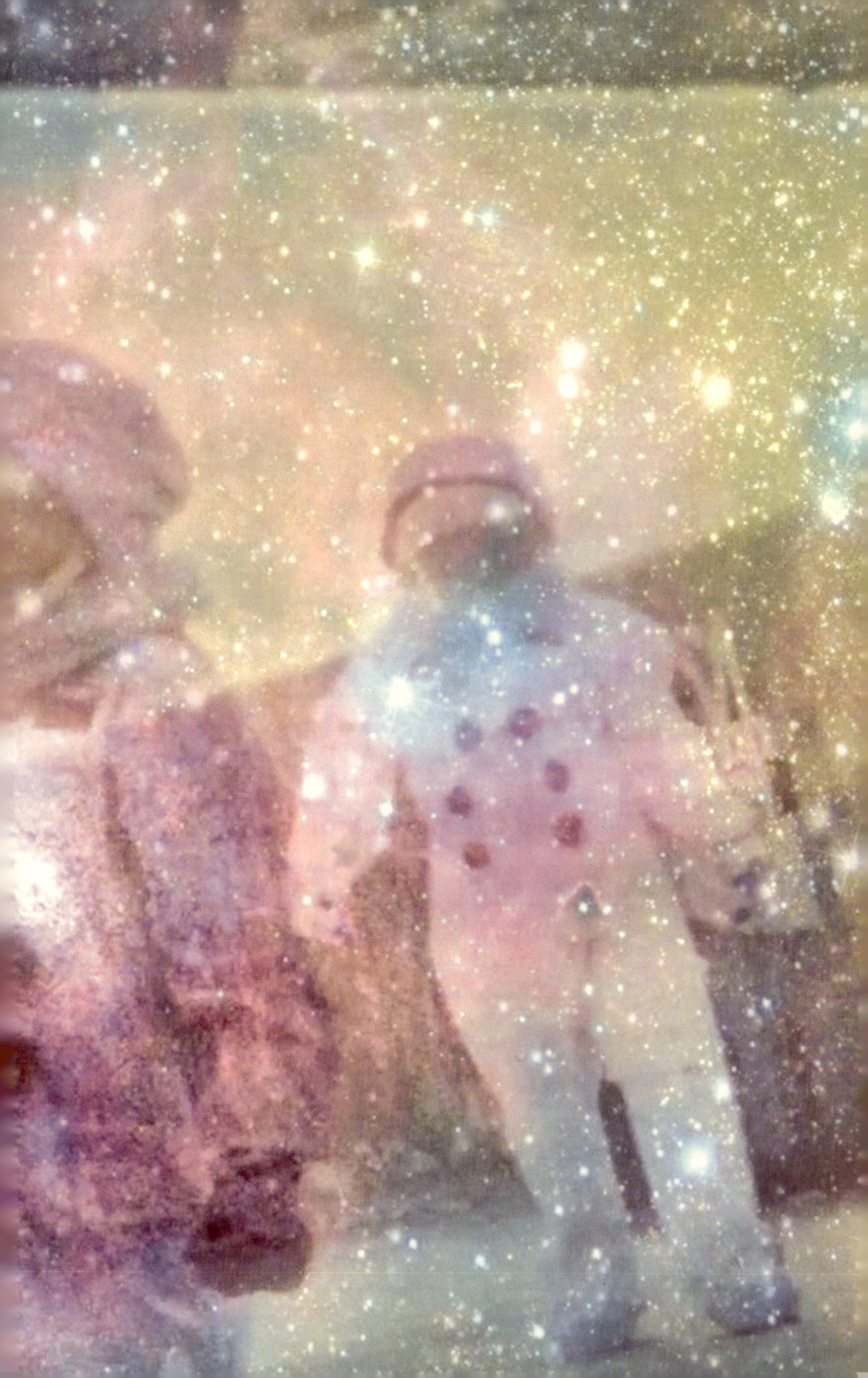

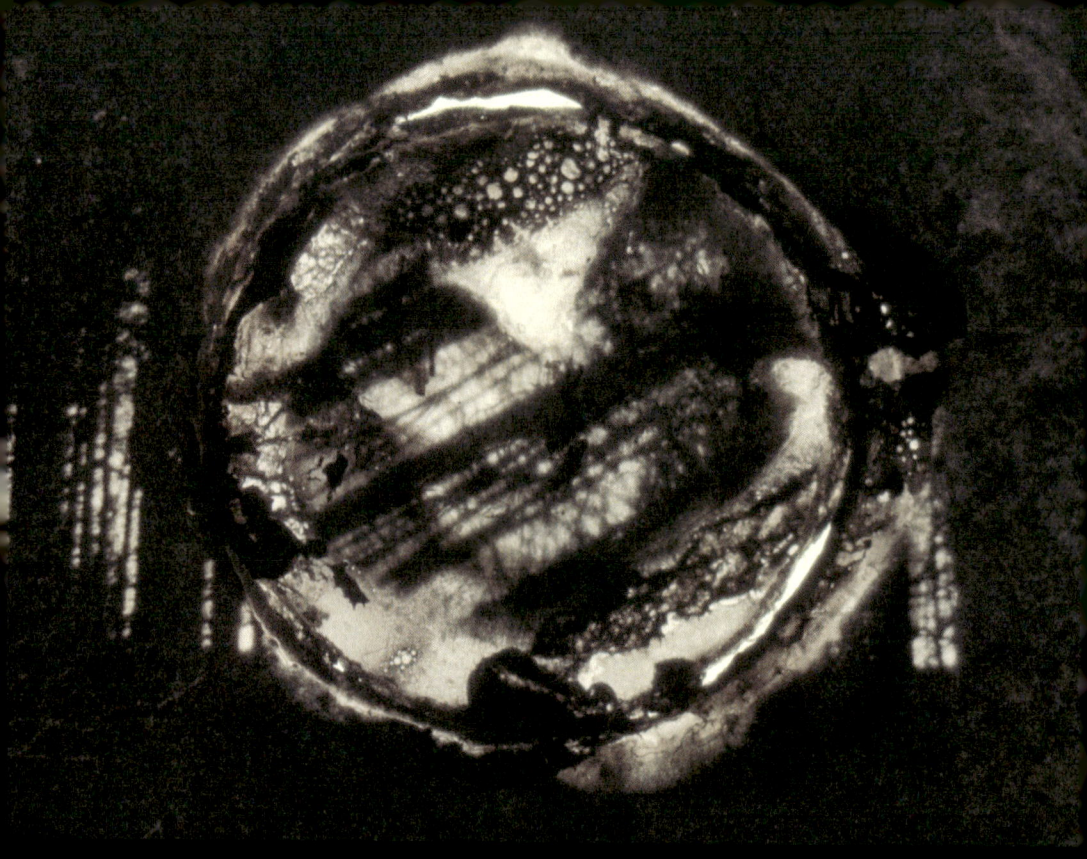

Autojektor//Basilisk

In April of 2019 I spent a couple of weeks in Germany's Black Forest taking 4 reels of b&w reversal super8 and a Sankyo cm-300. Each day involved a roughly 20km hike into the forests surrounding the town of Zell im Wiesental. It was during these off-trail hikes, when I would find myself lost in the choking dense woods, where I wrote and shot a short film called Basilisk.

In process the film would be pretty simple. I wanted a multitude of still frames that when played at 25 fps would create a violent barrage of trees. And tying them all together would be the motif of a single glaring eye.

So I started shooting. spending anywhere between 6-9 hours in the forest at a time. Single frame by single frame. And over the 14 days I left with 46 seconds of footage.

 When I got the processed film back, I used a leather punch with a 3mm diameter to remove a perfect circle from the centre of each frame. The removed piece was then painted with a thin layer of bleach around the rim – followed by another layer of black ink. This was also done to the area of the frame from which the circular piece was removed. Put back in place and secured with splicing tape.

Repeat for the next 1,144 frames.

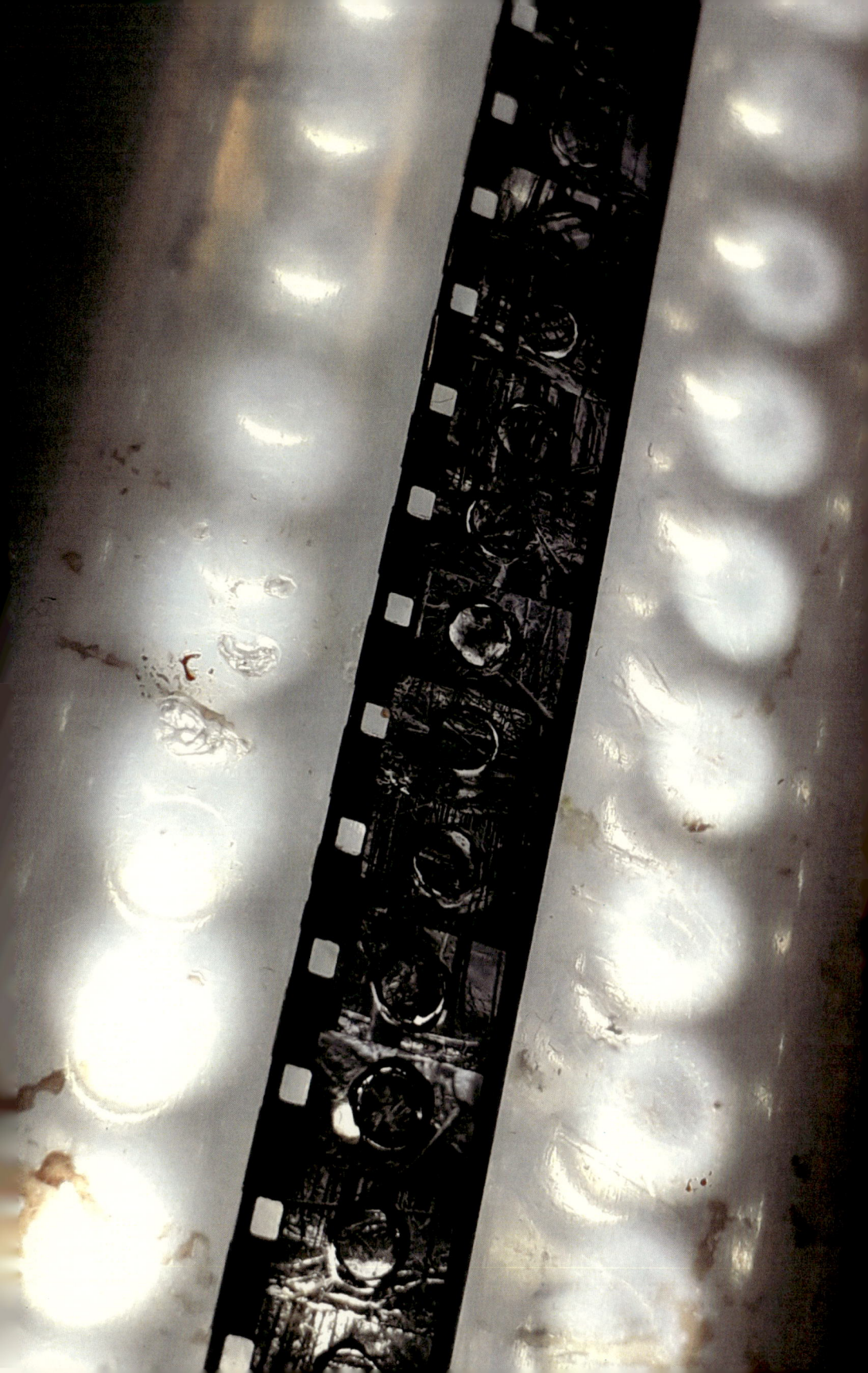

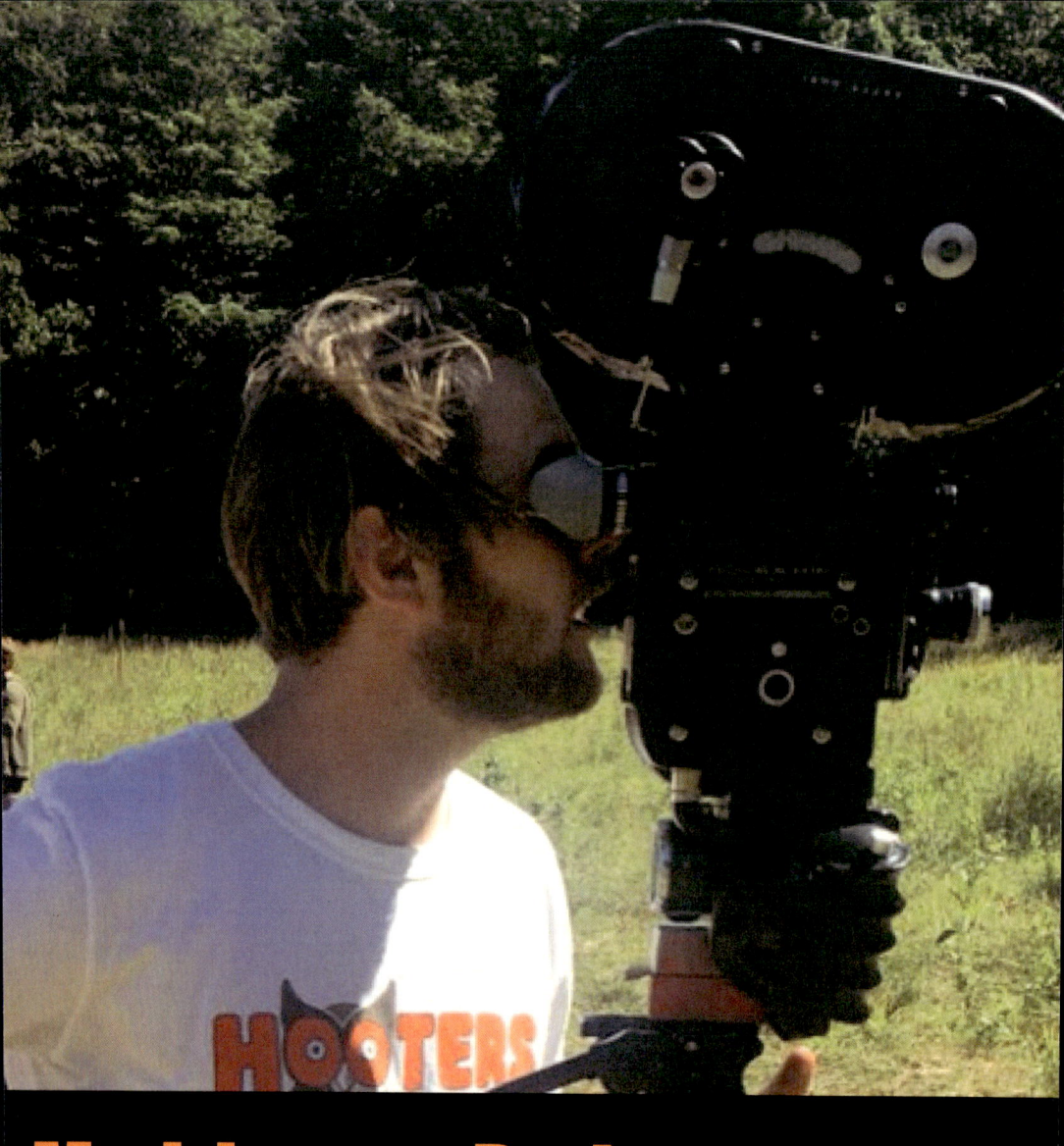

Making a Bolex EBM Adapter by Thomas Paul Wilson

The most common set up for the Bolex EBM is a handle grip and battery pack. It's a shooting at the hip set up but the camera does have a tripod connection on it which doesn't fit on modern tripods because of the fixed handle that gets in the way. The only option to shoot with this camera on a tripod is to own an old bolex tripod or find the other battery pack for sale without the handle which is uncommon.

I made an extension block for shooting my feature, which eliminated this problem and let me mount my camera to modern tripods with the run and gun handle set up. I used a block of aluminium to cut the weight down but mild steel will do. 55mm thick. 50mm wide. 95mm length.

Line one end of the block with the lip of the baseplate that is machine surfaced to avoid the 7 pin socket. Approximately 24mm from the edge of the block and lip is the centre for the tripod connection. Drill through the block as straight as possible with a 10mm drill bit. I used a pillar drill for accuracy but a steady hand will do the trick. Then counter sink the hole with a 20mm drill bit for the bolt head to sit flush with the block (as deep as it needs to be--keep checking).

For the bolt, the cameras thread on the baseplate is 3/8" witworth (BSW - British Standard Witworth) so you'll need to order 3/8" witworth bolt with a head at least 60mm in length to got through the block and reach the camera. If it's too long, cut and file down. The thread in the camera is only a few millimeters so be careful how much to take off with this part, keep checking and file down so it gets a good grip of the camera and fastens tight (the block shouldn't move).

Next you'll need to make a 2nd hole in the block and tap/thread the hole so your tripod baseplate will fix to the block (make sure your tripod is the larger 3/8" witworth connection and not the smaller 1/4" witworth to support the weight).

Approximately 41mm from the same edge you measured your bolt hole, you'll need to make your 2nd hole with a 8mm drill bit. Then tap/thread the hole with a 3/8" witworth hand tap at least 10mm deep to clear the tripod screw.

All of the tools can be picked up on eBay for a good price or check with a local hardware store. The price will be worth it for a still image.

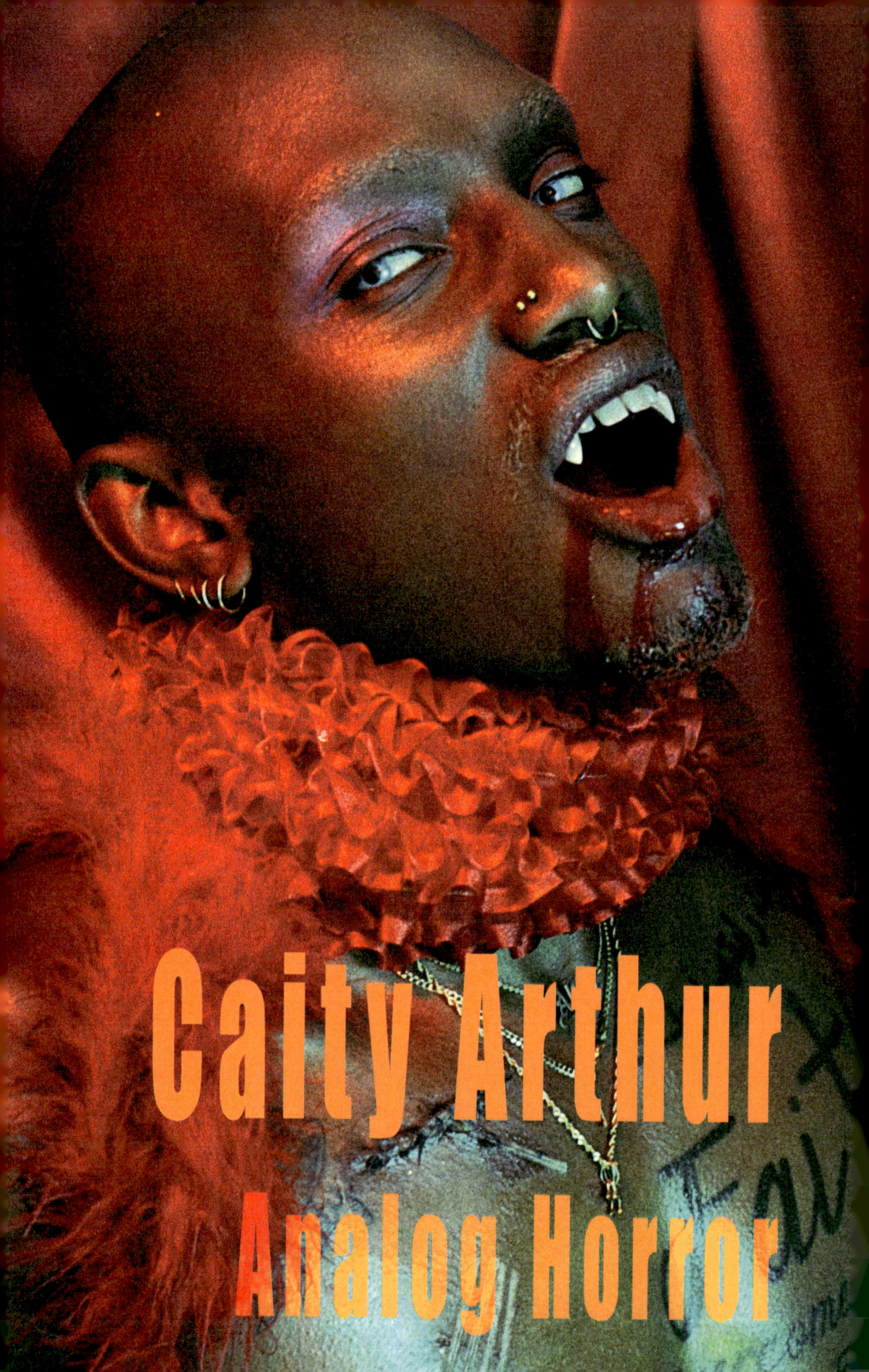

Thoughts On...

Caity Arthur is a multi-talented filmmaker who has worked as a producer at Buzzfeed and editor at Condé Nest, but its her love for gore, horror, and all things Halloween that has lead her to make several short film projects and film shoots shot on celluloid. Here are her thoughts on film.

On filmmaking roots:

I knew that I wanted to do film in high school. Before that, I was pretty gung ho on being an actor/dancer. My school actually ended up having a mandatory production class. I don't know what other high school does that's not specifically an arts high school, but for some reason my public school in Maplewood, New Jersey had a production class. I remember taking it and meeting some of my still current best friends in that class.

After High School I went to William Patterson University in New Jersey and studied Film there. When I graduated, I ended up moving back to Maplewood New Jersey, and hitting the pavement early. I was in New York probably every single day since the day that I got back from college in 2013. I literally would not stop going to New York, grabbing any internship gig I can possibly get my hands on. I was following around these bands for a while. I was doing everything I could possibly get my hands on. It was a little bit of a lonely time for me just learning how to do everything, but I wanted to be able to execute videos all by myself--from conceptualizing the idea to writing the script, to shooting, etc.

On working for Buzfeed:

Fast forward to my first gig, my first official gig, which was with Buzzfeed. I worked

with them full time for almost like three years and that's really where I honed in on creating, writing scripts, and pitching ideas to somebody. Halloween was my favorite time, because I'd be able to make all the Halloween content. I would aim for these overly ambitious projects. I was thankful for Buzzfeed. I learned to a lot on my own, but then I was able to polish my skills at Buzzfeed. I was working in an actual studio, setting up my own lights, being able to just do everything on my own still, but in a more professional setting.

On independent filmmaking:

A couple of years later I'm being creative at Buzzfeed, but I really wanted to create my own stuff. I'm going if I want to make my own horror film, which is the goal, and it's still the goal now, how am I able to do that? I had to go out on a limb, so I quit Buzzfeed, and I was scared shitless. I remember it to this day. I didn't even know what I was going to do. My mom really had my back in this moment and was just like, "you have to take the jump." But there was no way of me doing that unless I went freelance. After three years, I left Buzzfeed, and then I started creating my own stuff.

On the film *Bitten*:

I had a friend who is a composer. He knows how much I love horror, so he reached out to me and was like, "there's a film festival where videographers collaborate with people that compose music. You create the video, I create the sound, and then it gets screened." In a weekend I wrote this little script of this girl having a bad dream of being bitten. She wakes up and doesn't really understand where she is, doesn't understand what's going on, but she's bleeding from her shoulder. She goes outside, tries to figure out her situation and she runs into three people that are having a drink, having a good time. The male of the group goes up to her and tries to hit on her a couple of times, but she's transforming into a vampire. I shot it in a day, edited in a day, and then tried to send it to them that Monday, so it was a really quick. So that really made me really excited. Really made me happy. But I knew that I needed more, in terms of what I wanted and how I wanted to do this, so I, at that point, needed funds. I went to a job with Conde Nest.

On Shooting Film:

I love film. I love the way it looks, I've always been into really retro, old things. I was really lucky enough to in an early age, learn how to shoot with a Pentax and I loved the dark room process. My dad found a Super 8 camera, so I grab one of those, I bought a point and shoot, and I was just pretty much working out of a studio in Brooklyn called Holy Rad. I would leave Conde Nest at 6:00, then go straight to Holy Rad studio. I would shoot a bunch of rolls, and then record VHS or hi-8 tape. I was just recording friends and doing these photo shoots, doing their makeup really funky. I wanted to just be creative. I just started shooting some photos of my friends, and the more the I did that, the more these ideas came, and the more I started meeting new people, and I started really figuring out what I wanted to do.

On Aesthetics:

I started getting into doing my own makeup work and learning how to create scars. I am a big Halloween fan. I've been doing makeup for a while, but I really wanted to really hone in on SFX makeup. I started shooting my friends and doing their makeup, and then setting up sets. Creepy is my aesthetic. Dark is my aesthetic. But very analog and grainy. I just started working and honing in on what I wanted aesthetically, which is dark, bloody, queer--my own identity translated in my own photos,. I love horror, I love thrillers, I love gore.

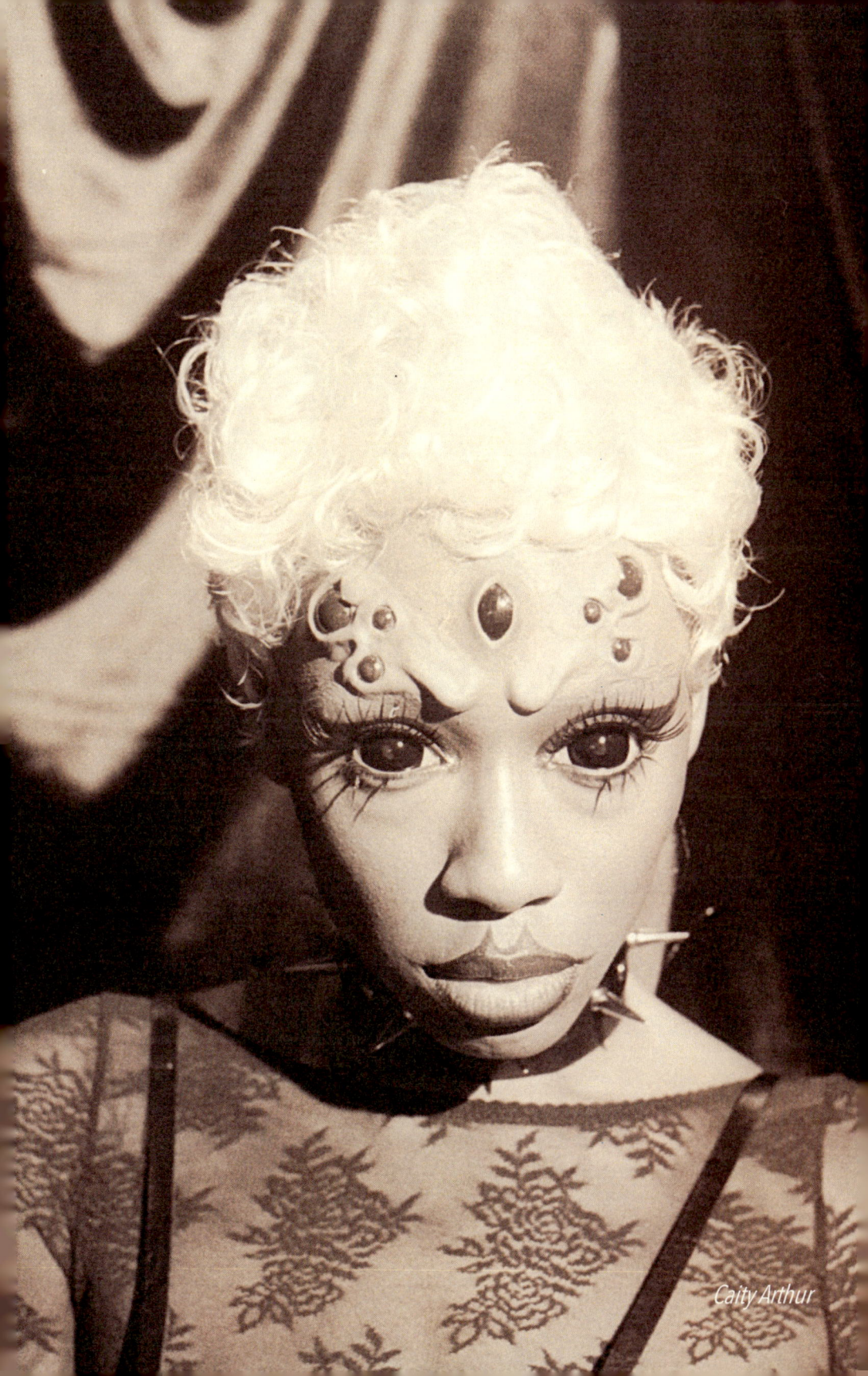

Caity Arthur

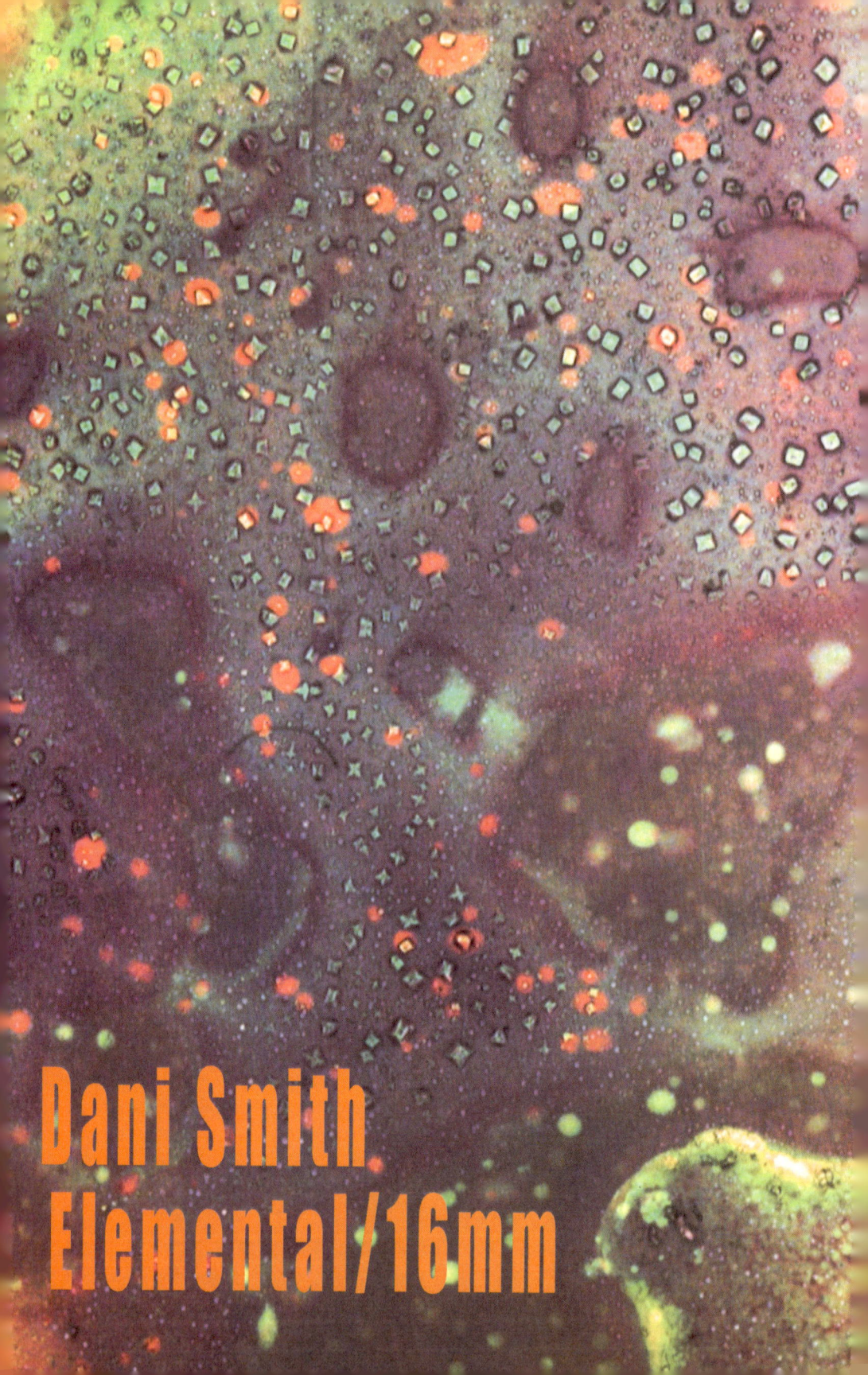

Dani Smith
Elemental/16mm

What inspired *Elemental*?

I took an Experimental Cinema course with Anna Kipervaser while working on my thesis project, a longer documentary about Northern Nevada and my family history there, when I was exposed to all sorts of works and techniques around direct animating and emulsion manipulation on 16mm film. I had been getting workprints made for my thesis film. I began experimenting with the leftover film as a sort of low-stakes creative outlet in the face of stressful and serious thesis work. I also learned how to make a contact print with a Bolex from a MONO NO AWARE workshop with Steve Cossman. Suddenly the combination of these two things-- direct animation and making multiple generations of the same footage, resulted in work that was not only visually exciting, but made conceptual sense in my broader thesis work about childhood memories, archival family movies, and homesickness.

Tell us about your process with *Elemental*. How did you decide to work directly with film?

Once I began playing with salt, dirt (from the Nevada desert), and bleach on some scraps of film, it was like a lightbulb turned on. The results were almost psychedelic in how vibrant and active the images became. I learned to hone this practice while experimenting with making Bolex contact prints of the same footage. Now I had generations of the same footage that I could further manipulate and each generation became more distorted, just like revisiting memories. The reason I was shooting much of my thesis documentary on 16mm film was because the physical 16mm film strip was a body that held information, much like the landscape of my upbringing. This side project became a more pure articulation of that idea of the film strip as an information-holding physical object, so the title *Elemental Correspondence* came from there.

What film stock did you use?

Most of the original footage was from workprints of footage shot on 50D, and some of the contact prints were made with higher speed color negative such as 250D that was cross-processed.

Can you tell us about your method for removing remjet?

It's a messy method! After processing I take the film on the Lomo reel into the bathroom where I spool it back onto daylight spools. Then, apologizing to a set of rewinds that are about to get soaked, I run the film back and forth on the rewinds in the bathtub. Six passes between the rewinds while sandwiching the film in a wet sponge seems to do the trick. I try to have room temperature water running from the bathtub faucet falling directly on the spool. Basically there's a lot of water and a lot of black remjet sprayed all over. I recommend taking a shower after this process so it doesn't stain your bathroom! Or at least cleaning as you go, because it gets messy. The film is then loaded back onto the Lomo for washing, photoflo, and then hung up to dry.

What other projects are you working on? Anything exciting coming up?

The architecture in Brooklyn has caught my attention, so I'm making a sort of flicker film composed of still images I've been capturing. I have plans for a short experimental film about Marilyn Monroe and some of her final years which were spent in the Reno area. Currently I'm submitting *Elemental Correspondence*, my thesis film *West From Ruby to Rose*, and other films made during my time in the MFA program to festivals. There are a lot of thoughts flowing through my mind and I am really trying to motivate myself to express my ideas through my work and to simply make.

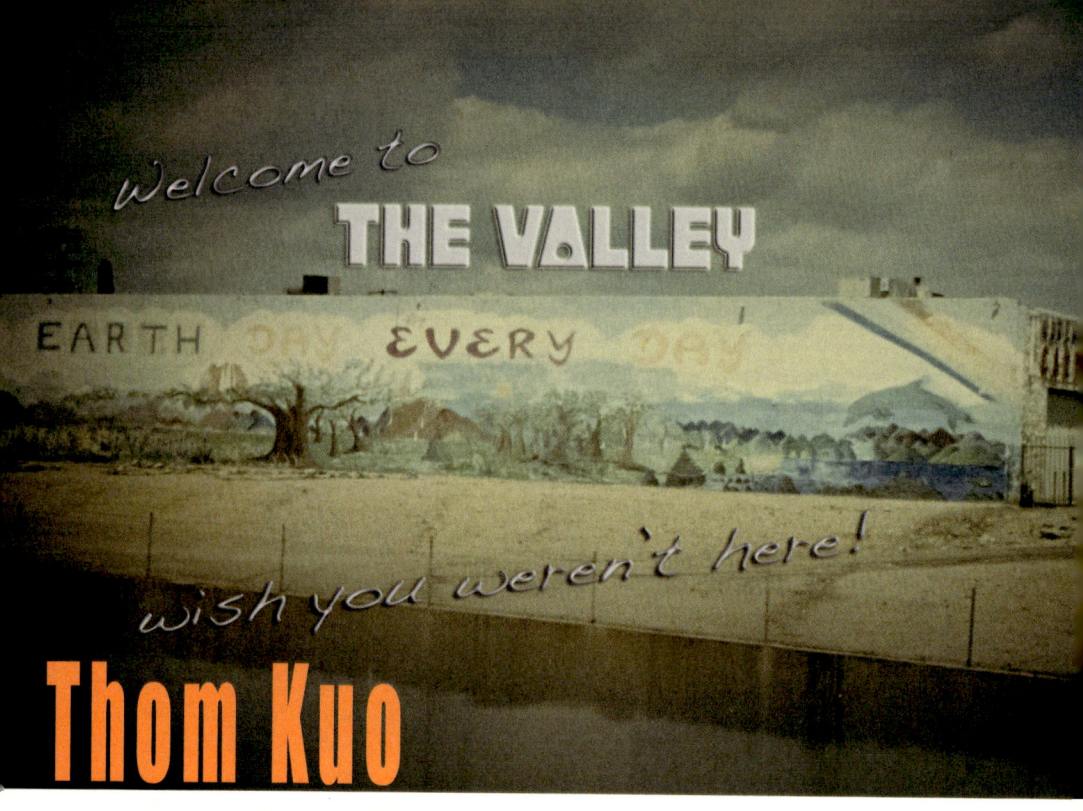

Thom Kuo

The Valley: Exquisite Corpse series

A detective goes in search of the killer of one of his informants and unravels a darker motive in the shadows of the San Fernando Valley.

The Valley series seems like an Exquisite Corpse for filmmakers. Can you talk about your process with the series?
Yes! That's the term! What a cool label "exquisite corpse". That's exactly what it is. I think when I was in high school we called it a fold poem. But this term is so much cooler. It started as an experiment where I could get people to shoot on film. I'd kick it off with the "pilot" then hand it off to a new writer and director and they'd continue the story. But take it to wherever they want to go. I discovered that, because the concept is a film noir, having a surreal quality to it was fine. There is a core story in "The Valley" (which is about a detective exploring the San Fernando Valley in search of a killer) but we've segued all over the place now. We've spun off the spin off. It's a tough juggle, but here's something really cool about making films with overlapping stories, you can use the same props and no one notices

you. You can say it was intentional! I'd solicited a few filmmaker friends, but they were busy. There were a couple of takers, but now I sort of use it as a film school to teach shooting on motion picture film. I give the production about $1000 and some film. I pay for processing and I transfer for them. Hopefully they get a great experience in shooting on film and that they're proud to use it on their reel. Or at the very least enjoy the process of filmmaking on actual film. The other stipulation is that they keep it to 3-5 pages which is why I call it a micro-series.

Why was it important to shoot 35mm?
We actually shoot on 35mm, regular 16mm, Super16mm on expired film, fresh film, Bolex, hand-cranked, it's a punk rock style. The pilot was in 35mm because it was all I had at the time and I had to use up some expired film

What camera and film stocks did you use?

Oh man, we used everything. Arriflex 35BL4, Arriflex 35-3, Arriflex SR2, SR1, Éclair NPR, Bolex, my friend's 2 perf Arriflex 35BL4. Is there a reason? Not really. With the exception of some handcranking footage which requires certain cameras, it's all just getting it filmed. For film stock every Kodak Vision stock and some really old EXR stock I can get my hands on. We use Fuji here and there, but there's a remjet issue I don't want to get into. Ha.

What's your favorite gear to work with?

I bought this Arriflex SR1 from a camera pawn shop a few months ago. It was a consignment deal where I don't think the shop knew what it was or cared. It has to be my favorite camera because it's so imperfect. Imperfection is beauty to me. I have to jostle the on/off switch to get it to work. As a curmudgeon camera tech once barked at me "it's not a propeller on a plane you have to jump start." I laughed. But, something about the broken down nature of the camera makes sense for "The Valley." It's an early model Arriflex SR that still has what they call the French circuit board. When it goes, it's toast. You can swap out for German parts but might as well buy a later serial numbered camera. No one with any brains would use it in confidence. So, here I am.

Favorite film stock?

Kodak Vision 3 500T. You can be the absolute most incompetent film shooter and STILL get something. If I were to go into the back catalog of Kodak film it has to be the Kodak EXR 100T. A LOT of people in the 1980's used that film stock which is why they look the way they do.

You scan film for a living for big studios. What's that like?

Because we deal with demanding quality, we've had to deal with what standards really are. In essence, scanning is giving a base to which all images moving forward will work off of. If that's the case, it needs to be at a place where everyone can agree on.

I do see a LOT of mistakes. And I can't report back to the powers that be who spend millions on their project that they should embrace the mistake. But with music videos or commercials, plenty of times I've spoken to people who felt the crushing defeat only to see the footage end up in 90% of the project. Hell, we use to purposely scratch film all the time. A director/DoP friend of mine sometimes lets me do it

still! I love it.

We're about to be in a whole new decade. Where do you see the future of celluloid filmmaking?

It has a resurgence because of the young people. Yes, the millennials which most people criticize, from what I've seen, have picked it up from the ground, and dusted it off for the next (at least) 20 years and I'm very grateful for them. Because their influences are based on what their parents exposed them to, they wonder why digital looks so flat and nothing like what the past looks like. I feel people inherently feel the difference, if they can't articulate it. They know the imperfections feel more real. An image that originates in digital doesn't have a pop that film has. Never will, regardless of what grain overlay you apply to it. It moves differently. And it will always be an algorithm.

Anything else you'd like to add?

There has NEVER been a better time to shoot film. Equipment is cheap. Film is cheap. Processing is cheap. And EVERYONE wants to help on a film project. They love the craft and want to see for themselves. Celluloid is an exquisite corpse, in a different way. Anyone who has shot or dealt with it, has added to it. And every experience with every moment will be unique. Think about this, that roll of film in your camera only belongs to your project. The amount of time it's been in the fridge or closet, to the time it goes through your camera, to the time of day you shot it at. That belongs to YOU. Granted, there is sometimes no consistency to this, but that's commerce, not art. It's beauty in alchemy. This is the closest we will ever get to real magic. I'm not trying to be pretentious by saying so. Because it's chemicals reacting with other chemicals to get an image. It still blows my mind.

But on a much more practical sense, celluloid is also archival. I just scanned some footage from the 1940's that someone had left in a vault. With the exception of film chatter and poor registration, it could come out of a camera today. That's longevity on a consumer level. Go out there and beat and batter and experiment with film. This isn't something people can do in digital on a physical level. What you get out is something much more beautiful than you can ever expect. Let the rest of the world deal with sterility.

Svava Valdis Tergesen's

Solarization Recipe

I came across this recipe by accident. I had never developed using a Morse tank before, and didn't realize that bleach times needed to be greatly extended when using this type of development tank. I ran through my normal development process (develop > bleach > exposure > final development) before I noticed anything was wrong. Horrified at the result and not wanting to lose my film, I plunged my film back into the bleach until I correctly bleached out the highlights and finished by re-developing again. The result was a ghostly solarized image.

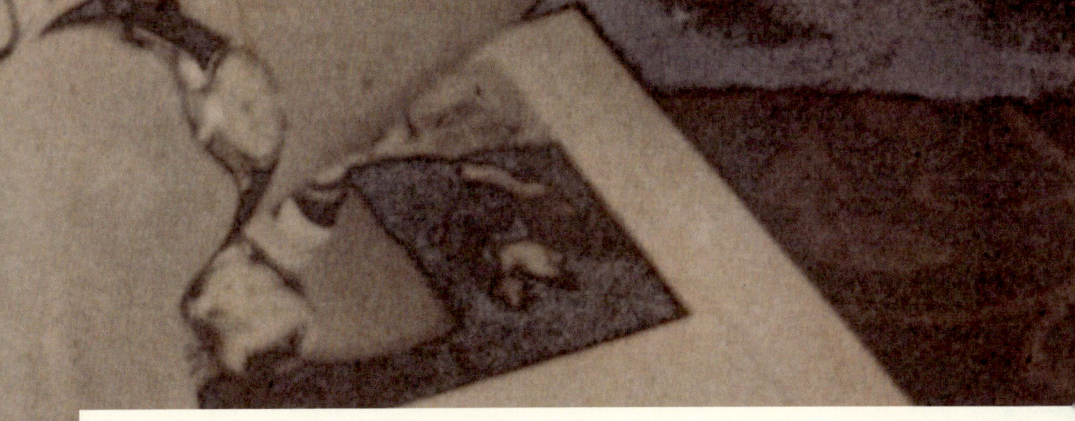

1. Develop film for 7 minutes in Morse tank at room temperature with normal agitation (should take about 1 minute for the film to pass from one reel to the next). I used Kodak Tri-X 7266 reversal BW film and D19 developer.

2. Proceed to wash film for 2 minutes.

3. Bleach film for 7 minutes, just enough so that the unexposed film turns yellow but the highlights remain as black silver metals. (Morse tank 7 minutes).

4. Wash 2 mins.

5. Exposure. Turn on all the lights and remove the tank lid. I opened the window cover and using my phone flashlight setting in front of the window, I passed the film through for several rotations. Keep lights on from now on.

6. 1st Re-development. Re-develop the film for 5 minutes, again turning evenly so that it takes 1 minute for the film to pass from one reel to the next.

7. 2nd Bleach. Next, re-bleach everything until no black silver metal is left on the film and image is clear/yellow. Turn very slowly, allowing the bleach to penetrate each section and inspecting often.

8. Wash.

9. 2nd Re-development. Develop until the shadows turn sufficiently dark. The shadows will not be as dark as with normal reversal processing.

note: Morse tanks work in such a way that only a small portion of the film is being exposed to chemicals at any given moment. The following times would need to be adjusted for if hand processing in a bucket, which allows for all parts of the film to receive equal access to chemicals at the same time

Britany Gunderson
Lining/16mm

Undressing the body while simultaneously being covered up, routine is discovered through obsessive tendencies.

Tell us about yourself.

Right now, I'm a senior in the film program at UW-Milwaukee. I make films and videos, as well as textile and other fine art works. I work in the 16mm film archive and 16mm film lab at UWM where I assist in running a film processing machine. For the past 4 years, I've also helped program and run the Milwaukee Underground Film Festival, which is super important to me and a huge part of my being. I've been listening to a lot of The Breeders and I'm currently reading Orlando by Virginia Woolf.

How did you come up with the idea for Lining?

Lining was a response to a class I was in called Sex & Gender in Film & Video. Initially, I had the idea of putting thread onto 16mm film, but wasn't really sure how it would work or what it would look like. I've been interested in textiles lately, as well as the feminine histories within them, and wanted to explore my idea through both textile and film mediums. I saw the dressing and undressing of a body as a routine thing, as something that defined a body, but also as something sexualized. Thread and clothes are a clear connection, while surface and use are revealed simultaneously on film - this was a gesture I was interested in. As I started to put the thread over the images of undressing, I realized that this was also about an obsessive tendency to cover everything up. I think Lining was a mixture of wanting to see what it would be like to perform for a camera and wondering what the image would really look like.

How did you incorporate thread within your film? Did the projector ever eat your film with all the layering?

To attach the thread onto my film I used double-sided tape and just stuck it on there, which worked for the most part! For every take, I'd added one more strand of thread, so the more undressed the body became on film the more the thread tried to cover it up. After all the thread was attached, I ran it through the optical printer and did front lighting - which is where I put a light in front of the film (in addition to the projection light in the back) so that it would light up anything on the surface of my film as it was rephotographed.

And YES, it definitely started to eat my film and do all kinds of things the thicker the thread got. On my first try, I actually had to start over and take some thread off because it was too much. In the middle of the film you can see the frame shifting and the thread piling up where it got jammed in the gate. The film would keep going but the thread would stay still, so I often had to help pull it through by hand.

Who are some of your artistic inspirations?

Joyce Wieland is a huge inspiration and not just in her films, but other works too. Also Rose Lowder, Betzy Bromberg, Sadie Benning, Jodie Mack, Charlotte Pryce, Nazli Dincel, Carolee Schneemann, Eva Hesse, Lenore Tawney.

What's next for you?

I'm working on my senior thesis film right now, which will be completed sometime in Spring 2020, and I'm planning on shooting and finishing on film. I've never finished a film on film, and I want to do it while I have all this access as a student. Content-wise, it's loosely based on the relationship I have with my mom, but it's still transforming. Textiles are incorporated into this one as well, as I'm making quilts and blankets and clothes that go along with it.

How do you like your film program?

I love it! It's like I couldn't have picked a better place for what I'm interested in and what I needed artistically. There's a heavy focus on experimental media, where nearly every class we're watching experimental films - it's a constant flow of media I never encountered before coming here, and the staff are all amazing filmmakers/artists/teachers. We have an archive of 16mm films (which I also work in) that are screened on film a few times a semester, so the programming is great. And there's all the equipment! I am extremely grateful to have access to this much 16mm film equipment - optical and contact printers, editing stations, projectors, cameras… and the film processing machine that I help run. It's such a hot-bed of analog and experimental film, and it really helped me in figuring out my own artistic process.

What do you want to do after you graduate?

Graduate school is something I'm interested in, but not entirely sure yet. I think I want to take a year-ish off of school before really considering that, but I mostly want to keep making films and see what it's like to make them on my own time. I also like setting up screenings and working at film festivals, so I'd like to try to do some type of screening series and travel around to festivals!

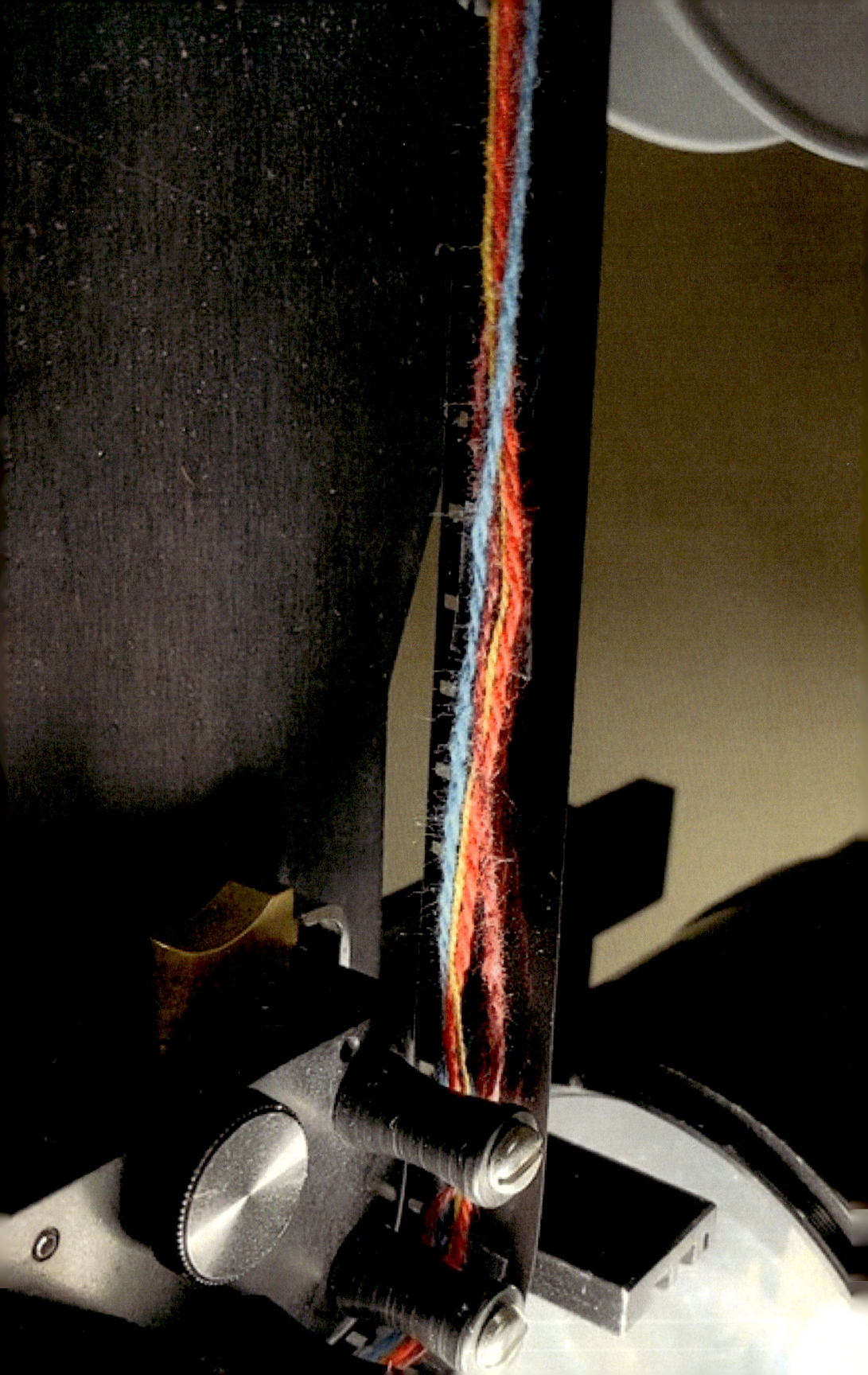

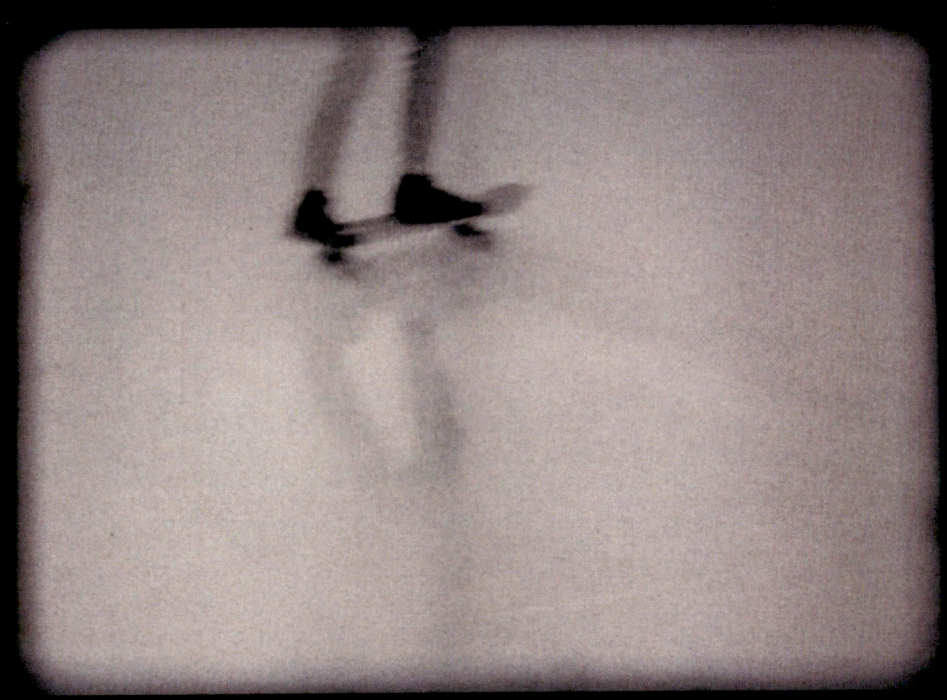

On Film Challenges:

"We participated the super-8 challenge, a program presented by a local film and video society called FAVA (Film and Video Arts Society of Alberta) we were given the tools and had a short deadline. i had just started getting into skateboarding, trying to devour its long spanning culture online in a summer and decided to make my own parody skate video of all the tricks I learned - which wasn't much. "

-Mona Fani

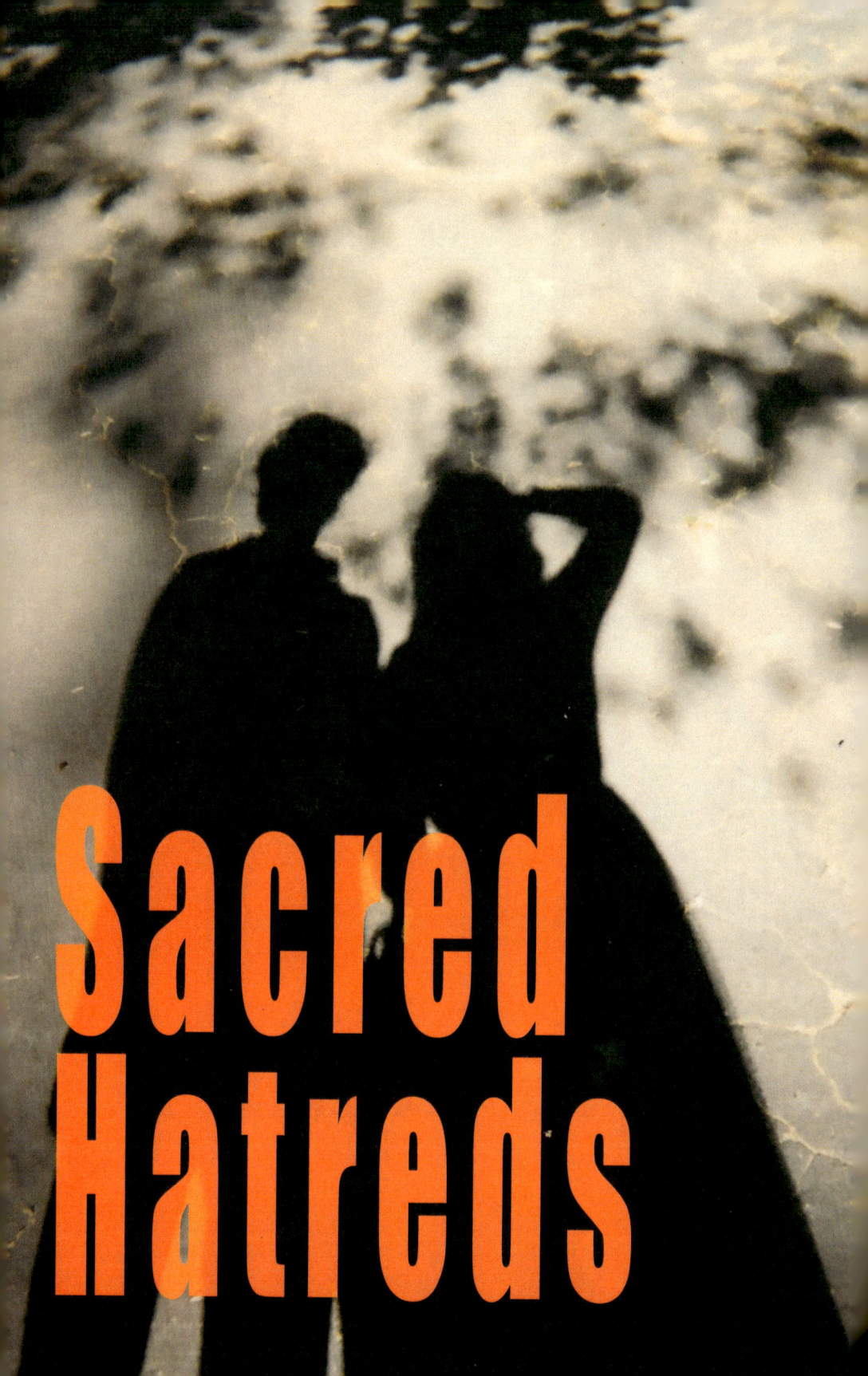

35mm Photography/Mixed Media

Tell us about your process.
I don't have rigid, concrete ideas when it comes to my work. I start off with vague ideas that create the framework, and from that point on I experiment and develop my ideas further. My flexible approach creates very endearing imperfections and pleasant surprises that are emblematic of my work, and I avoid creating restrictive and unrealistic expectations for myself because I know my work will never be perfect (and that's okay)!

What inspires you generally, or what inspired one or two of the pieces you've submitted?
I am currently heavily inspired by the medievalism in the Romanticist and Arts and Crafts movements, the D.I.Y. spirit of Dada and punk visual art forms, and the nostalgia and aesthetics of vintage films (I just watched Rosemary's Baby and I loved it).

What's the best piece of advice you've ever received?
I recommend watching *Bowl cut maintenance 1000* by hamishpatterson high frequency tribe on YouTube if you're ever feeling down. Trust me. It's a video of a surfer dude trimming his bowl cut while sharing philosophical gems such as "imperfection is the key to perfection".

What environmental factors are most helpful or limiting to your process?
The environmental shit-fest we're experiencing right now is shaping the way I create and view my art. I love collecting "junk" like tchotchkes from secondhand shops; paper, crafts, and packaging scraps from the trash; and dried flower bouquets. I hope to create less waste by giving these items a second life by incorporating them into my art. Tis mixed media approach also pushes me to add a 3-dimensional touch to my art by creating physical layers and mixing textures. I also strongly disagree with the fast-fashion business model, and so I have been experimenting with creating quilts and clothing items because I want to create functional art pieces that can be used for years to come.

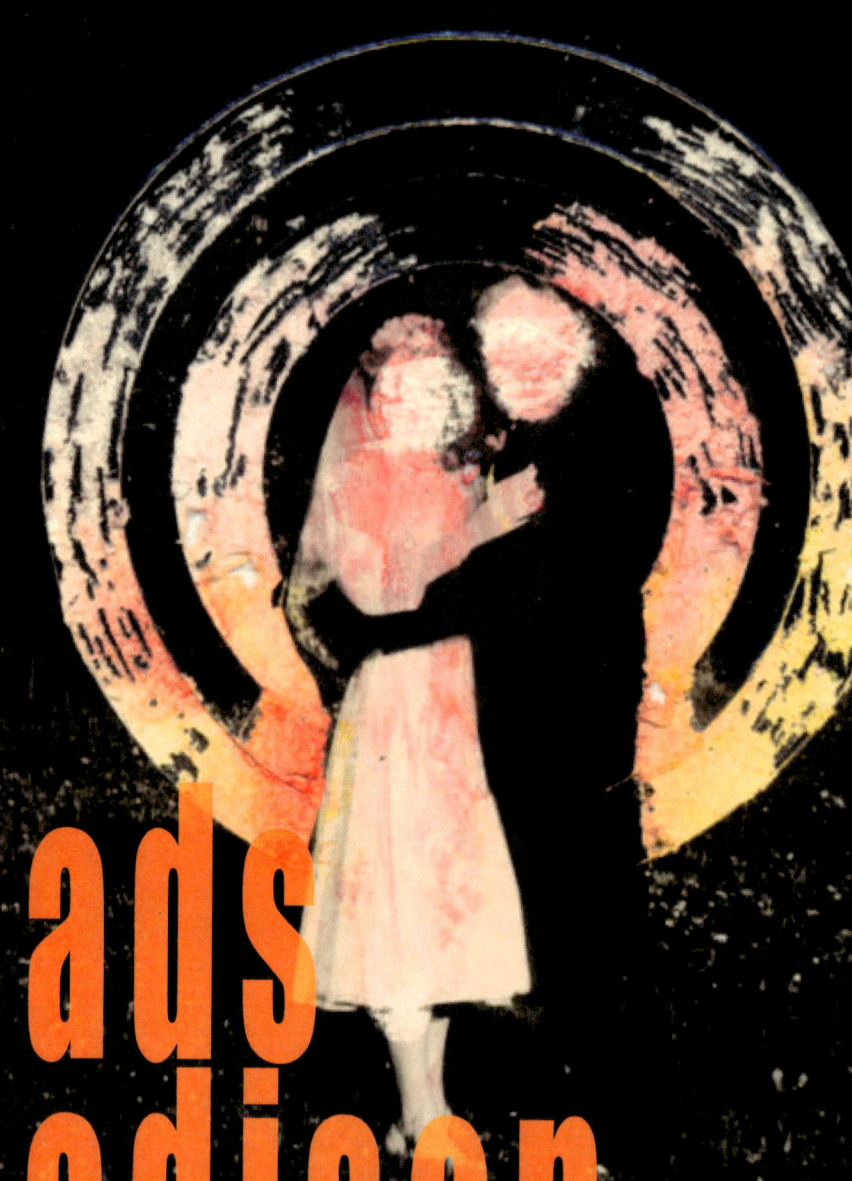

Mads
Madison

Wasted Films
Polariod/35mm/Etc.

Tell us about your process.
I mainly work with vintage/found/wasted fotage that I get at fleamarkets, the internet or via friend. So I actually don't shoot that much anymore, but talking about it makes me want to start again. I know how to do B/W film and paper developing, and I really love the intimacy it creates with prints. I love the creative options it offers. I did an entire series with a friend, developing paper in juice, mouthwash, milk, and other crazy stuff.

Film can be very unpredicatble. Tell us about a time when you learned or evolved from a mistake.
This is what made me do what I'm doing now. Nobody taught me how to shoot, I learned by trial-and-error. A lot of errors to be honest. So the wasted shots (film, prints, and Polaroids) kept piling up. That's when I started experimenting. And this made me more comfortable with shooting more, because I knew the 'failed' shots would be turned into something beautiful.

What inspires you generally, or what inspired one or two of the pieces you've submitted?
Everything inspires me, and then nothing inspires me. I love browsing through other artists' feeds, I like to test the idea of "what happens if I do this or that." Sometimes it's just a mood that makes me do things. Most of the time, there's not really a plan for what is going to happen. Maybe it's a gut feeling. I just pick a photo, look at my tools, and I start.

What's the best piece of advice you've ever received?
It would be easier to list all the bad advices I got. But what really helped me was the advice to look for gratification and happiness inside of me rather than listening to (negative) feedback or ideas of others.

What environmental factors are most helpful or limiting to your process?
The most limiting factor is the small room I work in, I hoard tools and old photos. Bits and pieces that might be useful on a collage. Besides that, I incorporate environmental factors. I froze photos in a block of ice and left them in a greenhouse in extreme heat.

Anything else you want to lay on us?
Don't let anyone force you to explain your work. Do what you do because it makes you happy. F*** negative feedback, nobody can tell you if what you're doing is good or bad.

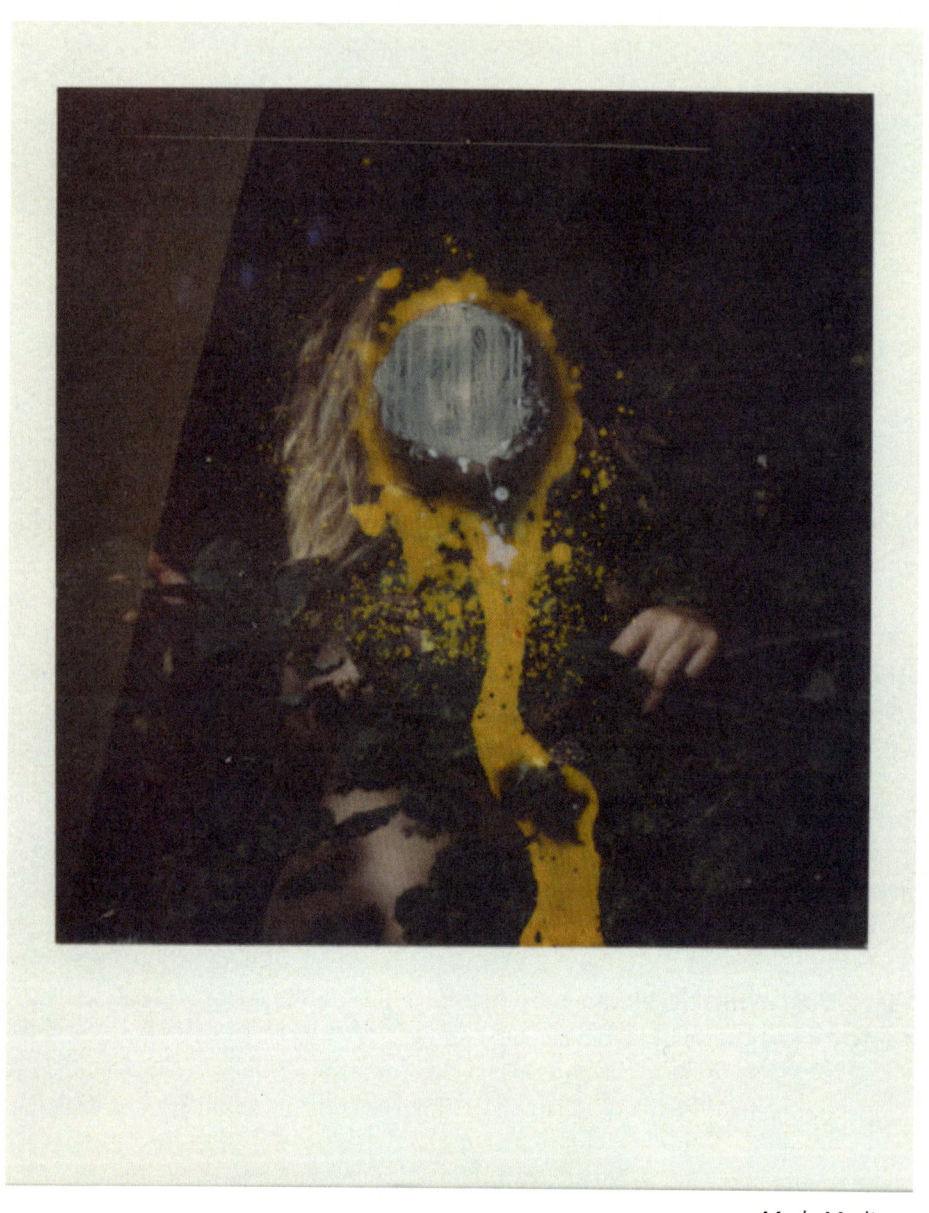

Mads Madison

"Amensia" is an experimental video art piece shot on mini DV by Shane Dedman. It is the genesis of their second solo show, forthcoming with TAR Project Residency at Day & Night Projects in Atlanta, GA in June 2020. Dedman has been exploring the concept of the archive since they read an article in Berlin based magazine 032c about the management of James Baldwin's archive, Derrida's *Archive Fever*, and discovering how inaccessible video art is within academic/institutional archives. The work focuses on documenting their ruined physical writing archive as a transformational experience of creating and maintaining new selves. Dedman harbors anxiety about the future, but they are persistent to use alchemy to change the tragic into forces of curiousity.

Amnesia

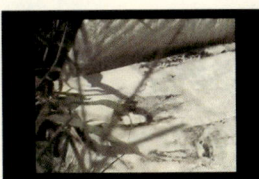 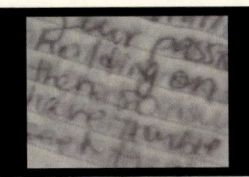 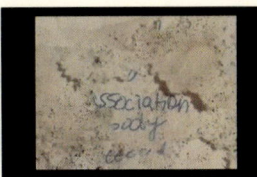

Stills from "Amnesia" by Shane Dedman

Amnesia Trascript:

All my earliest writings are gone;
The whispers of a child self were lost in a flood
As I waded in doubt on a foreign land, planning a new life.
They sat in a cedar box, left decaying as spores of black mold grew casually like a stain.
Each page, a transparent inkblot of conscious streams.
Their contents were surface soot of a malleable mind,
A disembodied prance on the cliff predicating the mark of permanence.
I brim with the desire of obstinance but flow freely to an unmarked grave.
Did I ever exist if not of entombed document?
In that form, I no longer exist; I can no longer look back on the document.
What transpires to the page, arranged in sequence but in moment may no longer render truth.
An archive exists not as truth but as proof.

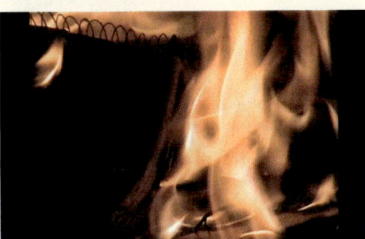 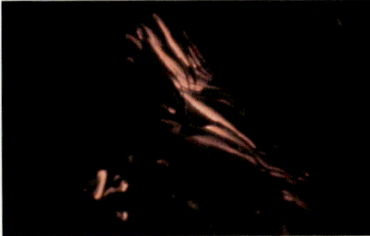

Stills from "Archive on Fire" by Shane Dedman

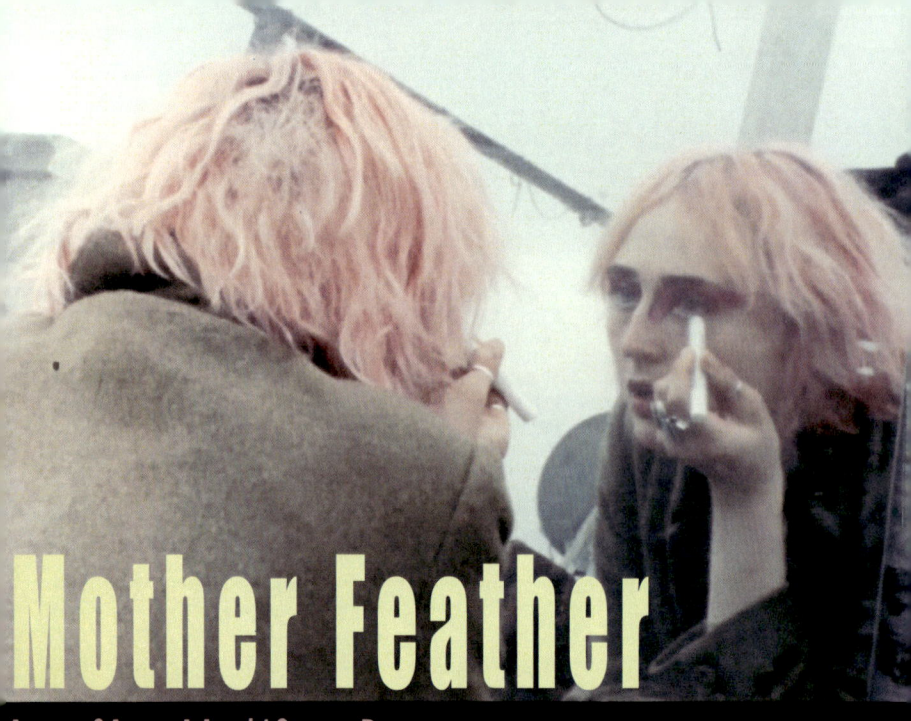

Mother Feather

Jess Giacobbe/16mm Documentary

How did the documentary on Mother Feather come to be?

This mini-doc began while taking a filmmaking workshop with MONO NO AWARE in Brooklyn, NY. I had been wanting to revisit film for a while. It had been an almost a 5 year hiatus for me. I knew that I would be shooting in color and I knew I wanted to capture the striking costume and make-up of the band, Mother Feather.

What film stock did you shoot on? Do you have a favorite film stock?

I shot on Kodak VISION3 250D 16mm Color Negative with a Bolex RX-5. To be honest I haven't explored shooting on other film stocks outside Kodak, but I can say I truly enjoyed shooting color. I found that color can be more visceral in telling a story, especially around the idea of costume and identity.

You projected live work with Mono No Aware. What did you project and what was it like projecting on film?

Sadly, I was unable to make it to the screening!. This piece, Mother Feather, was projected amongst other projects created through MONO. But seeing your own work projected is so vivid and beautiful and nerve wracking all at the same time. Projection

is performative. You do not have the same sense of ease as when you press play on a digital file. So many scary and amazing things can happen when showing something live.

I read that you came from a fine art background before filmmaking. How did those two worlds collide?

I began art school and thought I knew exactly what I wanted to major in, then quickly realized I had no idea what I wanted to do. This led to me studying multiple disciplines simultaneously. Early on, in a sculpture course we were prompted to create a performative response to our pieces. I had little technical filmmaking knowledge, but decided to make a film anyway. I began learning the medium through performance documentation, simply experimenting, and going with my gut. I still think this was an advantage at the time, I was totally uninhibited and fearless when making this first film. I believe that I took risks early on that I wouldn't have if I went on the traditional filmmaking trajectory. After this project I decided to focus on film/digital video and took as many classes as I could during my undergrad years. Coming from a fine arts background, I think thats why I gravitated toward more experimental filmmaking. Thankfully I attended a university that still taught 16mm

DO

TRULY

ESIRE?

Charlie Mirador

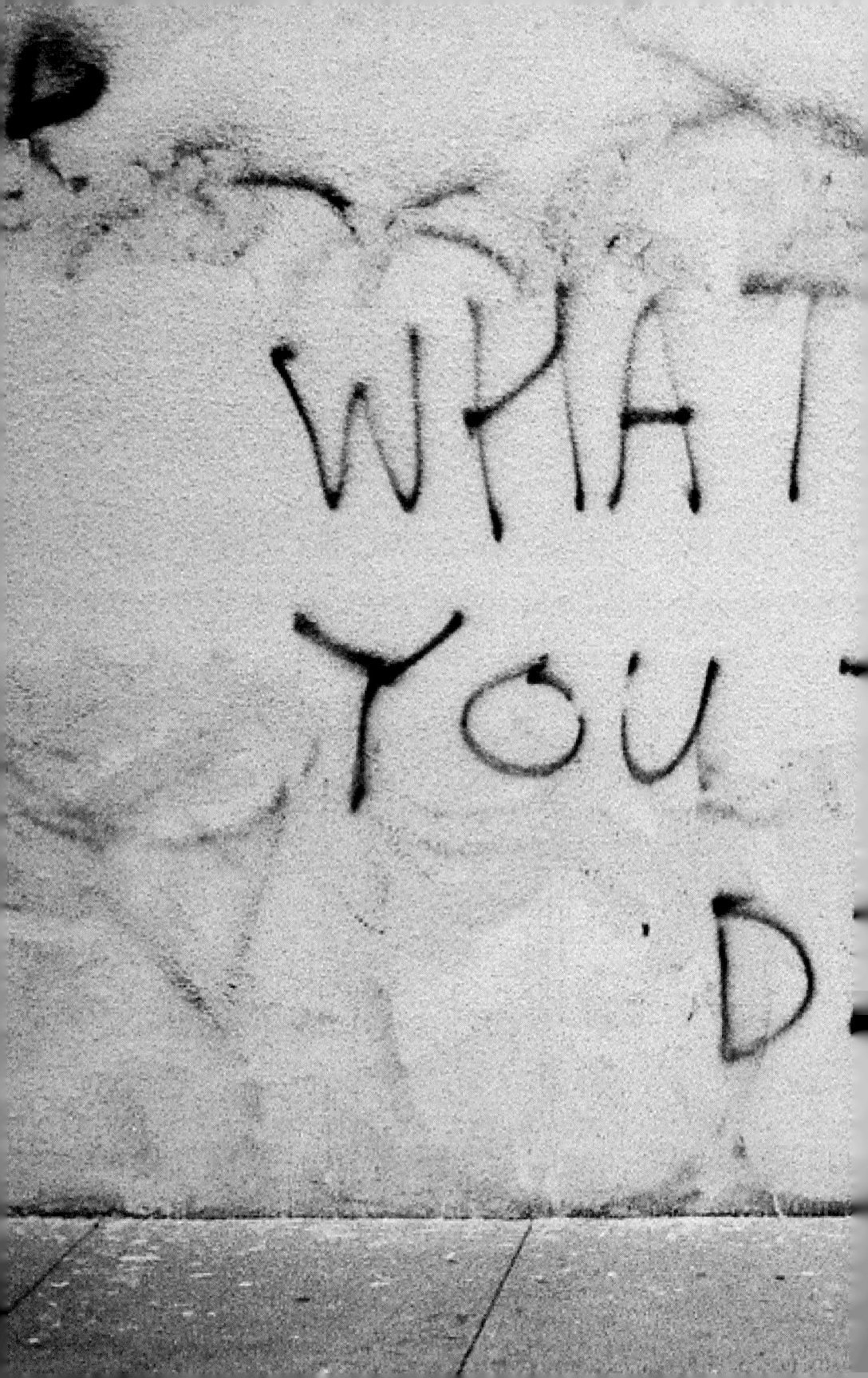

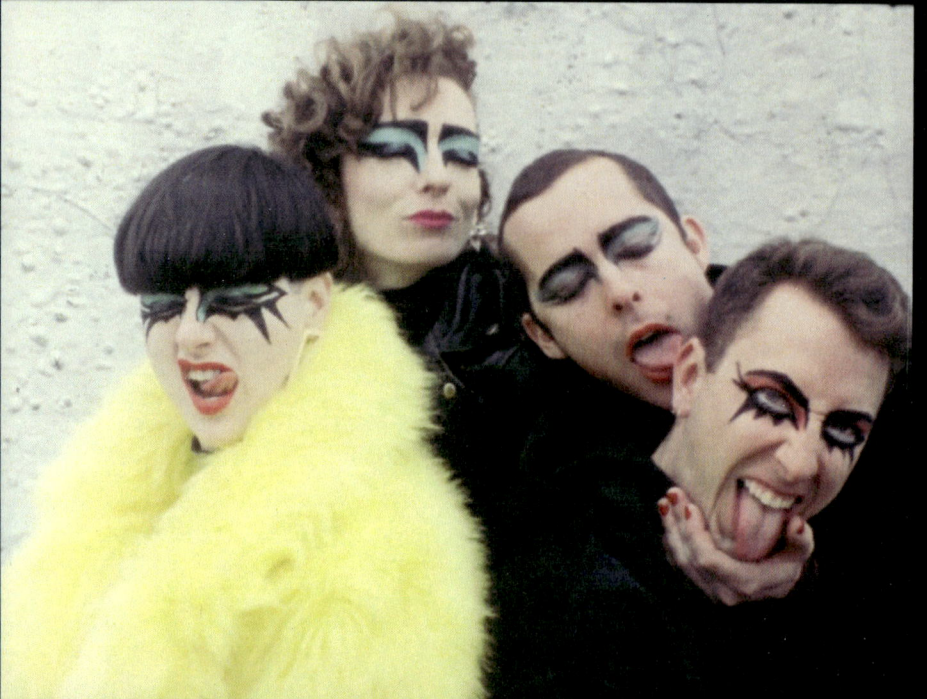

You run Oscillation Transia Film Festival, a festival that uses solar power to project films. How did that start?
Oscillation Transia Film Festival started as an idea in 2016. I knew I wanted to start a traveling film festival that would host screenings in outdoor and sometimes off-grid locations. I placed an open call online seeking films for this event that didn't even exist yet, and overnight I had already received nearly two dozen submissions. I was visiting Austin Krause, a good friend at the time, who happened to be a solar engineer and wanted to get behind this idea. The two of us jumped in head first to get OT off the ground. In the spring of 2017, we hosted our very first fundraiser and successful kickstarter campaign. This gave us the boost we needed to literally get this show on the road. Now, Oscillation Transia Film Festival is a fourth-year non-profit, hosting free outdoor solarpowered showcases of independent cinema and solar energy education across America. My personal focus in this project is to share innovative independent and experimental films across the U.S. I encourage, and am honestly biased to filmmakers who submit work created on film. Thus far, we have only shown digital transfers of analog work, but our goal is to start hosting live projections in 2020.

16mm filmmaking often evokes nostalgia. I noticed a lot of your work deals with memory and place. I'm wondering if you can talk a bit about how you grapple with using a nostalgic medium?
AGREED! I feel that whatever you shoot on film begins to feel timeless, and easily nostalgic. This topic hits home and is exactly what I struggled with when creating my undergrad thesis and work thereafter. The conundrum was to not weigh my work with nostalgia. I came to a realization and conclusion that I needed to reinvent the term entirely. I had to think of it as a positive feeling that could build potential from an existing memory. I try to think of nostalgia as an opportunity to reconfigure a memory or a place, or even discover something new in a topic so heavy. I definitely still grapple with it, even in mediums outside filmmaking.

What do you want your audience to walk away with after seeing your film?
I'd like my audience to appreciate the preciousness, look, feel, and grittiness of work on film. Also, to have a newfound respect and curiosity for the metal band Mother Feather, they are truly badass.

Anything else to add?
Film is certainly not dead. Shout out to MONO NO AWARE in NYC who are constantly offering workshops, screenings, and community events around film.